# POWER NG
# BUS NESS

The First
100 Years
of Eaton
Corporation

Celebrating
100 YEARS
Ideals that Endure

# POWER NG
## BUS NESS

The First
100 Years
of Eaton
Corporation

### Jeffrey L. Rodengen
Edited by Elizabeth Fernandez
Design and Layout by Sandy Cruz

Opposite: As Eaton has evolved from a components manufacturer to a leading provider of diversified power management solutions, it has maintained a strong focus on quality. Shown here in 1984, a computer-controlled probe, accurate to one ten-thousandth of an inch, inspects one of Eaton's viscous converter clutches.

Write Stuff Enterprises, LLC.
1001 South Andrews Avenue
Fort Lauderdale, FL 33316
**1-800-900-Book** (1-800-900-2665)
(954) 462-6657
www.writestuffbooks.com

The publisher has made every effort to identify and locate the source of the photographs included in this edition of *Powering Business: The First 100 Years of Eaton Corporation*. Grateful acknowledgment is made to those who have kindly granted permission for the use of their materials in this edition. If there are instances where proper credit was not given, the publisher will gladly make any necessary corrections in subsequent printings.

**Publisher's Cataloging-In-Publication Data**
*(Prepared by The Donohue Group, Inc.)*

Rodengen, Jeffrey L.

 Powering business : the first 100 years of Eaton Corporation / Jeffrey L. Rodengen ; edited by Elizabeth Fernandez ; design and layout by Sandy Cruz.

 p. ; cm.

 Includes index.
 ISBN: 978-1-932022-48-3

 1. Eaton Corporation—History.  2. Machinery industry—United States—History.  3. Automobile supplies industry—United States—History. 4. Power (Mechanics)—Technological innovations—History.  I. Fernandez, Elizabeth. II. Cruz, Sandy.  III. Title.

HD9705.U64 E264 2011
338.7/6218/0973          2011923629

Completely produced in the United States of America
10 9 8 7 6 5 4 3 2 1

## Also by Jeffrey L. Rodengen

*The Legend of Chris-Craft*

*IRON FIST:*
*The Lives of Carl Kiekhaefer*

*Evinrude-Johnson and*
*The Legend of OMC*

*Serving the Silent Service:*
*The Legend of Electric Boat*

*The Legend of Dr Pepper/Seven-Up*

*The Legend of Honeywell*

*The Legend of Briggs & Stratton*

*The Legend of Ingersoll-Rand*

*The Legend of Stanley:*
*150 Years of The Stanley Works*

*The MicroAge Way*

*The Legend of Halliburton*

*The Legend of York International*

*The Legend of Nucor Corporation*

*The Legend of Goodyear:*
*The First 100 Years*

*The Legend of AMP*

*The Legend of Cessna*

*The Legend of VF Corporation*

*The Spirit of AMD*

*The Legend of Rowan*

*New Horizons:*
*The Story of Ashland Inc.*

*The History of American Standard*

*The Legend of Mercury Marine*

*The Legend of Federal-Mogul*

*Against the Odds:*
*Inter-Tel—The First 30 Years*

*The Legend of Pfizer*

*State of the Heart: The Practical Guide*
*to Your Heart and Heart Surgery*
*with Larry W. Stephenson, M.D.*

*The Legend of Worthington Industries*

*The Legend of IBP*

*The Legend of Trinity Industries, Inc.*

*The Legend of*
*Cornelius Vanderbilt Whitney*

*The Legend of Amdahl*

*The Legend of Litton Industries*

*The Legend of Gulfstream*

*The Legend of Bertram*
*with David A. Patten*

*The Legend of Ritchie Bros. Auctioneers*

*The Legend of ALLTEL*
*with David A. Patten*

*The Yes, you can of Invacare*
*Corporation*
*with Anthony L. Wall*

*The Ship in the Balloon:*
*The Story of Boston Scientific and the*
*Development of Less-Invasive Medicine*

*The Legend of Day & Zimmermann*

*The Legend of Noble Drilling*

*Fifty Years of Innovation:*
*Kulicke & Soffa*

*Biomet—From Warsaw to the World*
*with Richard F. Hubbard*

*NRA: An American Legend*

*The Heritage and Values of RPM, Inc.*

*The Marmon Group:*
*The First Fifty Years*

*The Legend of Grainger*

*The Legend of The Titan Corporation*
*with Richard F. Hubbard*

*The Legend of Discount Tire Co.*
*with Richard F. Hubbard*

*The Legend of Polaris*
*with Richard F. Hubbard*

*The Legend of La-Z-Boy*
*with Richard F. Hubbard*

*The Legend of McCarthy*
*with Richard F. Hubbard*

*Intervoice: Twenty Years of Innovation*
*with Richard F. Hubbard*

*Jefferson-Pilot Financial:*
*A Century of Excellence*
*with Richard F. Hubbard*

*The Legend of HCA*

*The Legend of Werner Enterprises*
*with Richard F. Hubbard*

*The History of J. F. Shea Co.*
*with Richard F. Hubbard*

*True to Our Vision: HNI Corporation*
*with Richard F. Hubbard*

*The Legend of Albert Trostel & Sons*
*with Richard F. Hubbard*

*The Legend of Sovereign Bancorp*
*with Richard F. Hubbard*

*Innovation is the Best Medicine:*
*The extraordinary story of Datascope*
*with Richard F. Hubbard*

*The Legend of Guardian Industries*

*The Legend of*
*Universal Forest Products*

*Changing the World: Polytechnic*
*University—The First 150 Years*

*Nothing is Impossible: The Legend*
*of Joe Hardy and 84 Lumber*

*In it for the Long Haul:*
*The Story of CRST*

*The Story of Parsons Corporation*

*Cerner: From Vision to Value*

*New Horizons:*
*The Story of Federated Investors*

*Office Depot: Taking Care of Business—*
*The First 20 Years*

*The Legend of General Parts:*
*Proudly Serving a World in Motion*

*Bard: Power of the Past,*
*Force of the Future*

*Innovation & Integrity:*
*The Story of Hub Group*

*Amica: A Century of Service*
*1907–2007*

*A Passion for Service:*
*The Story of ARAMARK*

*The Legend of Con-way:*
*A History of Service, Reliability,*
*Innovation, and Growth*

*Commanding the Waterways:*
*The Story of Sea Ray*

*Past, Present & Futures:*
*Chicago Mercantile Exchange*

*The Legend of Leggett & Platt*

*The Road Well Traveled:*
*The Story of Guy Bostick and*
*Comcar Industries*

*The Legend of Brink's*

*Kiewit: An Uncommon Company:*
*Celebrating the First 125 Years*

*The History of Embraer*

*Parker Hannifin Corporation:*
*A Winning Heritage*

*AECOM: 20 Years and Counting*

*A Symphony of Soloists: The Story*
*of Wakefern and ShopRite*

*JELD-WEN: Celebrating 50 Years*

*Innovation, Passion, Success:*
*The EMC Story*

# TABLE OF CONTENTS

# INTRODUCTION

BY

## ALEXANDER M. "SANDY" CUTLER

CHAIRMAN AND CEO

© 2007 ROGER MASTROIANNI

EATON CORPORATION HAS A VERY storied and proud history. It is the evolution of a deeply principled organization that has changed and grown through innovation, customer based market awareness, and manufacturing excellence. To choose a single word, I would say that Eaton has always had a great deal of *courage* to do the right thing, to make the necessary changes, to continue to learn, and to achieve great results.

Over the past century, as you will understand reading this record of Eaton's success, it is obvious that Eaton has changed a great deal in the products which we manufacture and in the markets that we serve. Eaton has always been a forward-looking company that has capitalized on its history and ability to transform itself into a dynamic and contemporary world-class enterprise.

Unchanging, however, are the core values which have sustained Eaton through two World Wars, the Great Depression, and the periodic recessions which

have tested the resiliency and foresight of a long line of leadership. From the founders themselves, to the companies which have joined Eaton along the way, there has been a tremendous focus on doing business right, reinforced by a strong culture of care for the individual employee and an unshakable commitment to our customers. Throughout the world, we recognize that our employees are our greatest asset, and the source of the ingenuity and determination that has made Eaton's success possible. Power is ultimately produced by a vibrant culture.

This strong foundation of a values-based culture has provided our company with the ability to foster dramatic innovation and change while preserving our commitment to the highest level of values. Early in this past decade, the company was again able to utilize our strong values-based culture as the launching pad for three fundamental changes in the aspirations and achievements of our company. First, we raised our aspirations to grow our earnings at 15 percent per year through the economic cycle. Second, as an important element of capturing this accelerated rate of growth, we embraced a basic change in our operating style—becoming an integrated operating company. And third, we built our market focus around the theme of power management.

Eaton continues to adapt and change, reflecting the ongoing changes in the world in which we live and do business. We have improved our mix of businesses, greatly enlarged our business global footprint, and better balanced our ability to grow and maintain strong levels of profitability throughout the economic cycle. In this past decade, we have divested businesses and product lines which comprised approximately 20 percent of our revenues at the beginning of the decade—moving out of lower growth and less profitable businesses into ones with greater potential. More than 55 percent of our sales are now to customers outside the United States, in stark contrast to only 20 percent at the beginning of the decade, with approximately 25 percent of total sales now occurring in the fast growing emerging economies of the world. And our revenues are now well balanced through the early, middle, and late segments of the global economic cycle—providing both our shareholders and employees with a far more stable operating environment and financial results.

When J. O. Eaton founded the company in 1911, he had a vision about a transformational axle for the fledgling trucking industry. He saw a megatrend—the explosion of the transportation industry—and he had the courage and conviction to innovate and bet on that megatrend. One hundred years later, the company he founded is fueled by these same convictions: the courage to look forward and spot the megatrends that will fuel our growth and profitability, the ability to conceptualize and innovate, the capability to produce products and services with outstanding quality and world-competitive costs, and the conviction to serve our customers both in original application and in their aftermarket and service requirements.

Today, Eaton is the global leader in power management solutions, delivered by more than 70,000 talented employees throughout the world, and serving customers in 150 countries. This year, we celebrate our first 100 years in business. From all of us, thank you for helping us mark this special milestone.

# ACKNOWLEDGMENTS

MANY DEDICATED PEOPLE ASsisted in the research, preparation, and publication of *Powering Business: The First 100 Years of Eaton Corporation.*

Research Assistant Laura Putre conducted the principal archival research for the book, while Executive Editor Elizabeth Fernandez managed the editorial content. Senior Vice President/Creative Director Sandy Cruz brought the story to life.

Several key individuals associated with Eaton provided their assistance in development of the book from its outline to its finished product, including Don McGrath, Earl R. Franklin, Tim Weidner, Peter Gerber, and Cheryl Young. A special thank you goes to Sandy Cutler for contributing the book's introduction.

All of the people interviewed—Eaton employees, retirees, and friends—were generous with their time and insights. Those who shared their memories and thoughts include: Alfonso B. Acevedo, Revathi Advaithi, Craig Arnold, Domenico Bertolino, William W. Blausey, Stephen M. Buente,

William E. Butler, Frank Campbell, Randy W. Carson, Arnaldo Comisso, Susan J. Cook, E. Mandell de Windt, William B. Doggett, Richard H. Fearon, Jeff Finch, Earl R. Franklin, Gerry L. Gherlein, Thomas S. Gross, Stephen R. Hardis, William C. Hartman, Richard D. Holder, Jake Hooks, J. Robert Horst, Larry Iwan, C. B. Kim, Gary D. Klasen, Jeffrey M. Krakowiak, Jean-Pierre Lacombe, Eli Lustgarten, Joe Massey, Robert J. McCloskey, James W. McGill, Mark M. McGuire, John R. Miller, John S. Mitchell, Bradley J. Morton, Thomas W. O'Boyle, Larry M. Oman, Joe Palchak, Victor A. Pelson, Al Rankin, Billie K. Rawot, Ken D. Semelsberger, James E. Sweetnam, Gary L. Tooker, Yannis P. Tsavalas, William R. VanArsdale, Ted Wheeler, Jerry R. Whitaker, and Joseph L. Wolfsberger.

Finally, special thanks are extended to the staff at Write Stuff Enterprises, LLC: Joseph Demma, Elijah Meyer, graphic designer; Roy Adelman, on-press supervisor; Lynn C. Jones, proofreader; Barbara Martin, Patti Dolbow, and Mary Aaron, transcriptionists; Donna M. Drialo, indexer; Amy Major, executive assistant to Jeffrey L. Rodengen; Marianne Roberts, president, publisher, and chief financial officer; and Stanislava Alexandrova, marketing manager.

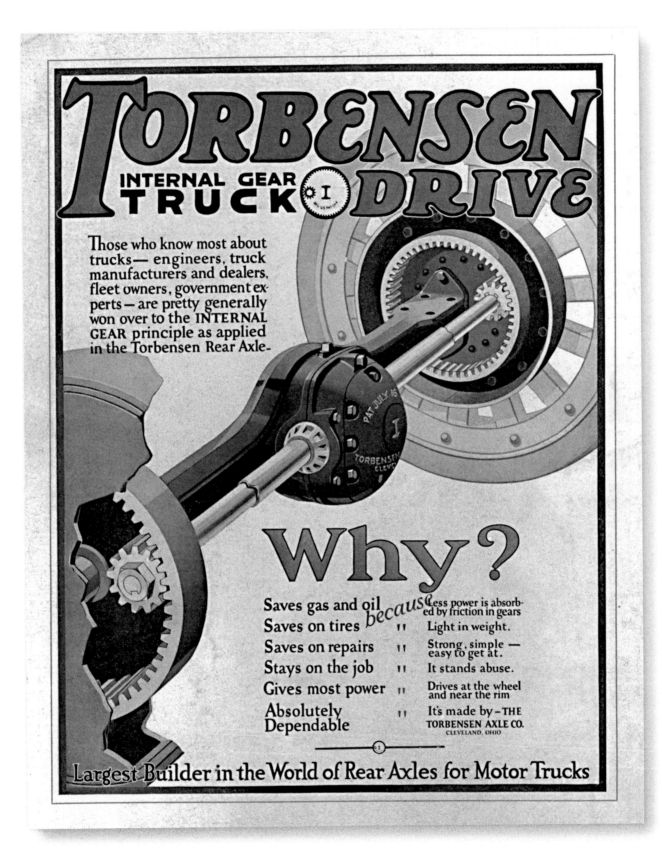

A 1918 advertisement emphasizes the fact that Torbensen's internal gear-driven truck axles gave the most power in the industry with the least amount of gas usage and the best resistance to wear and tear.

## CHAPTER ONE

# WHEELS IN MOTION

## THE EARLY YEARS

*The coming of the automobile has literally changed the face of the earth.*

—*New York Times*, 1913[1]

INNOVATORS IN GERMANY AND FRANCE built the first automobiles, but it was their American counterparts who were the first to introduce motorcars to a mass audience.

The first successful motor vehicle propelled by a gas engine was produced in the United States in 1893.[2] Interest in the "horseless carriage" reached fever pitch two years later, when accounts of the Paris–Bordeaux automobile race spread to American shores. Impressed by the fact that nine of 22 vehicles managed to complete a 727-mile course, U.S. entrepreneurs and inventors rushed to build and market their own versions of the automobile.[3]

Automotive manufacturing began in earnest in Cleveland in 1896, when self-taught bicycle manufacturer Alexander Winton constructed an internal-combustion engine and built a car with a 2-cylinder, 2-horsepower engine that could reach speeds of 12 mph. He demonstrated his handiwork to a group of Cleveland reporters later that year, generating considerable excitement. Also in 1896, the Winton Motor Carriage Company was formed, employing a tinsmith, blacksmith, painter, trimmer, two woodworkers, seven machinists, and three helpers. To promote the company, Winton drove his product from Cleveland to New York—a trip that took 10 days and helped generate about 20 new orders for the company's cars.

By 1897, Winton began manufacturing a standard car model— a milestone in automobile history. Previously, all American cars had been individually made to order.[4]

Cleveland had an advantage over other cities in the manufacture of automobiles because it had a thriving bicycle manufacturing industry, and automobiles used similar components such as chain-and-sprocket drives, wire-spoke wheels with rubber tires, frames made of tubular steel, and rearview mirrors, easing the transition for bicycle manufacturers such as Winton.[5]

Meanwhile, in Brooklyn, New York, Danish-born machinist Viggo Torbensen began developing an internal gear-driven axle while working as the foreman of the De Dion-Bouton Motorette Company. An aspiring engineer, by 1900 Torbensen had served as a supervisor for the Philadelphia subway system, started and sold a steam yacht firm, and spent two

An early logo for Torbensen Gear & Axle.

years in Germany studying automobile manufacturing. He saw a need in the industry for a simple axle that could handle the toughest conditions, including heavy loads, extreme terrain, exposure to the elements, and wear and tear from frequent use. His idea was to use a shaft instead of a chain to transmit power from the axle to the wheel. "My invention is especially useful for motor trucks where the parts are heavy," he wrote in his application letter to the U.S. Patent Office.[6] He recognized that truck component engineering varied tremendously from that of passenger cars, "with the necessity for enormous power to be concentrated in the driving wheels at certain times."[7]

At the time, motorized trucks were just being introduced into the U.S. market. By 1901, the country had a mere 7,000 cars and 141 hard-surface roads (out of 2 million roads overall). However, many early pioneers had already recognized the potential of the powerful vehicles. Renowned author H. G. Wells predicted that truck fleets would soon eclipse railroads as a method of carrying cargo cross-country, with "the organization of large carrier companies using such motor trucks to carry goods in bulk or parcels on the high roads."[8]

## The Torbensen Axle

Torbensen built his first truck axle in his shop in 1902, which, he wrote, "could not properly be called a factory although the completed axles we

This building housed the operations of Torbensen Gear & Axle Company in Bloomfield, New Jersey, in 1911.

turned out were ... carefully machined and properly put together."[9]

By 1907, Chicago held the nation's first motor truck show. An automobile manufacturing company called Autocar stopped making automobiles and switched to 1½-ton trucks.[10]

Torbensen struggled to finance production of his axle until 1911, when he collaborated with a young entrepreneur named Joseph Oriel Eaton to form the Torbensen Gear & Axle Company. A graduate of Williams College in Massachusetts, J. O. Eaton had found success in the men's clothing business, cofounding the Interstate Shirt and Collar Company in Troy, New York. However, he instantly recognized the possibilities in Torbensen's new truck axle.

To bankroll the start-up, Eaton sold $45,000 in stock to his brother-in-law Henning Taube. That year, 10,681 trucks were manufactured in the United States. "There were few truck manufacturers to take our truck axles, so the only way we could be sure of disposing of them was to put together the completed truck by buying the rest of the parts, and then selling the whole machine," J. O. Eaton explained.[11]

In those days, the shop built the axles entirely from scratch, manufacturing only seven its first year. "It was 'hard sledding' because practically all parts of the axle had to be dug out of the raw material by ourselves with few special tools and no machinery to help us," wrote Torbensen in the first company newsletter. "There were no parts or accessories for sale which we could use. We were sustained by the belief that the automobile truck was the coming thing, and that the next few years would see phenomenal growth in the hauling industry."[12]

The growth did not come as fast as Eaton and Torbensen expected. They had felt trucks would catch on before passenger cars, considering trucks a necessity and cars a luxury. However, before World War I, the country simply did not have the infrastructure to support truck transport. During the prewar era, wrote Mark S. Foster in his book *A Nation on Wheels*, "road-building efforts in the United States were uncoordinated and ... largely ineffective." The general public perceived interstates as frivolous "'peacock alleys' which primarily served wealthy Americans with too much leisure time on their hands."[13]

## Welcome to Cleveland

The truck industry continued to grow in the period between 1911 and about 1913.[14] In 1912, Packard built the first truck to cross the country on its own power—a promising development.[15] However, the truck industry faced a slowdown soon afterward.

While the company produced 244 rear axles in 1913, by 1914, production had slowed to 175 a year.[16] Fortunately, Torbensen and Eaton had not overextended themselves, and the fledgling company was able to survive the slump. The pair moved the factory to Newark, New Jersey, for a short time, occupying "increased floor space" in a building for start-up manufacturing firms.[17]

They soon realized, however, that the center of the automobile industry was destined to be in the Midwest. Michigan was home to 75 auto manufacturers in 1911; Ohio ranked second with 63, including Winton, White, and Packard.[18]

J. O. Eaton decided to move the company to either Cleveland or Detroit. Cleveland quickly became the center of luxury automobile manufacturing, with new firms such as Peerless and Stearns introducing fancy models targeted toward the leisure class.

However, in Detroit, Henry Ford had a different vision—a car for the average person. In Detroit, according to historian John Rae, business leaders were willing to invest in huge factories with assembly lines for mass production.

J. O. Eaton was still mulling over the move when his wife, Edith, told him she "clearly preferred the amenities and lifestyle of Cleveland."[19] Her preference was a deciding factor.

The company moved to Cleveland in 1915, contracting with Columbia Axle Company to build Torbensen axles for the first year.[20]

Unable to keep pace with the sheer volume of cars the plants in Detroit could produce, Cleveland's boutique carmakers quickly faded, and Detroit became the capital of the automobile industry. However, Cleveland's entrepreneurs found another niche, shifting their focus to manufacturing parts for mass-produced vehicles.

Along with valve manufacturer TRW and car battery company Willard, Torbensen Axle was at the center of a thriving parts industry in Cleveland beginning in the 1910s.[21]

The company's business picked up after the move. The Columbia plant manufactured 1,889 Torbensen axles in 1915, more than 10 times the previous year's output.

Above: J. O. Eaton served in the New York Volunteer Infantry during the Spanish-American War.

Below: The Ford Motor Company, one of Torbensen's first customers, used Torbensen axles on its 1911 Ford pickup.

# J. O. EATON

JOSEPH ORIEL EATON, THE founder of Eaton Corporation, was known in Cleveland's business community for his integrity, quick mind, and grace under pressure. Although he was the son of a prominent portrait painter and attended an elite private college, he did not grow up in a privileged household. His father, J. O. Eaton Sr., died two years after he was born. He was raised by his widowed mother and his grandmother in Cincinnati, where he excelled within public schools and earned a scholarship to the prestigious Williams College in Massachusetts.

While in college, he held a series of odd jobs to make ends meet, including summer jobs as a bank clerk and writing a $5-a-week tennis column for the *Cincinnati Enquirer*. He once spent a day selling cigarettes on Broadway in New York City, but quit after he actually sampled his wares and realized no one was buying them because they tasted absolutely awful.[1]

J. O. Eaton also worked as an $8-a-week clerk for American Express in New York. "There were 124 other men in the same office doing the same monotonous work I did," he

## A New Factory and a Dedicated Workforce

After the company's early success in Cleveland, work began on a new Torbensen Axle plant on Cleveland's East Side, at 1115 E. 152nd Street, while general offices remained at Columbia Axle. "An overnight growth in truck demand … sent us scurrying around for enlarged facilities to meet it," Viggo Torbensen recalled.[22]

White Motor Company was a major Cleveland-based truck manufacturer and an early Torbensen Axle customer. It ceased production of automobiles in 1918 to focus solely on trucks. This photo shows the first White light steam truck, which was manufactured in 1900. *(Photo courtesy of Cleveland Public Library Photograph Collection.)*

recalled. "But I differed from them in two respects. They all chewed tobacco. I didn't. And they were content to stand still. I wasn't."[2]

After college, he enlisted in the Army, serving as a private with the New York Volunteer Infantry during the Spanish–American War. At the end of the war, he landed a job in Troy, New York, at George P. Ide & Co., shirt and collar manufacturers, where he was soon promoted to department manager.

In 1903, J. O. Eaton moved to Bloomfield, New Jersey, to work as an assistant general manager of the Empire Cream Separator Company. A year later, he founded the Interstate Shirt and Collar Company—where, he later joked, he "lost his shirttail."[3]

However, J. O. Eaton did not leave New York behind completely. He continued to return to Troy to date a young widow with four children named Edith Ide French—the daughter of his former boss, George Ide. J. O. Eaton and Edith married in 1910.

According to his 1949 obituary in the *Cleveland Plain Dealer*, J. O. Eaton saw such potential in Viggo Torbensen's two-speed axle for trucks that he rounded up $120,000 in investments to start Torbensen Axle. After the firm moved to Cleveland in 1915, "Eaton rapidly gained a reputation for financial and administrative ingenuity."[4]

He sold his interest in Torbensen Axle to Republic Motor Truck in 1918, only to buy back the company with a group of investors at Otis and Company investment banking firm, where he worked as a partner from 1921 to 1931.[5]

Although his greatest successes came in the field of truck and automobile manufacturing technology, according to *The History of Eaton Corporation*, he was "not a mechanical genius in the mold of Edison or Ford. In fact, he never learned to drive a car. He tried to drive one of the early electric models, rammed it into a wall, and never drove again."[6]

However, what he lacked in mechanical aptitude, he made up for in managerial skills. J. O. Eaton was known for his ability to inspire his loyal and devoted workforce and his attention to quality and detail in all aspects of business. When he died in 1949 at age 75, Eaton Corporation had become one of the five largest producers of automotive parts in the world, and J. O. Eaton was widely admired for his company's integrity in every aspect of its operations.[7]

The plant opened in 1916 as the Torbensen Axle Company and manufactured 10,068 rear axles in its first year as an Ohio corporation. The company also manufactured front axles for the first time, selling 989 in the first year alone. Large customers included the Republic Motor Truck Company, Olds Motor Company, Towmotor Company, International Harvester, Graham-Dodge, and Commerce. U.S. Postal Service trucks were also built with axles made by Torbensen Axle.[23]

Howard Markt, a writer for one of the industry magazines, marveled at the plant's efficiency, compared to other manufacturing concerns at the time. Rather than simply tossing scrap metal on the floor to be swept up later, shop workers sorted scrap into separate bins for chrome-vanadium steel, chrome-nickel steel, and malleable scrap. Heavy loads were lifted and lowered on platforms, and electric trucks transported materials

In 1915, Torbensen Axle established its first Cleveland headquarters in the Columbia Axle Company offices on Euclid Avenue.

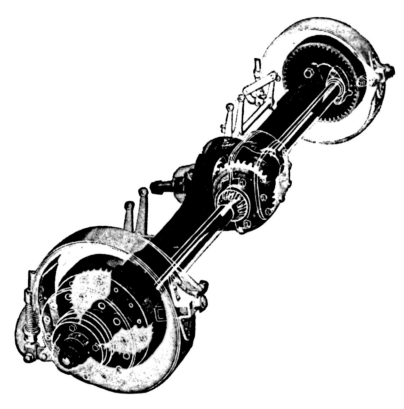

Above: This phantom view of the Torbensen Axle appeared in the company's 1918 newsletter, the *Torbensen Internal Opinion*.

Below: Cleveland was home to Stearns, a prominent manufacturer of luxury automobiles from 1898 to 1929. This photo shows the Stearns factory at the corner of Euclid Avenue and Lakeview Road in Cleveland.

around the plant. This system of stacking parts on platforms, rather than storing them on the shop floor as was common practice at the time, provided optimal working space for machine operators.[24]

The factory itself was smartly designed, Markt noted. Conduits for the plant's fuel, air, water, steam, and gas were contained in a tunnel that ran through the length of the shop, simplifying inspection and repairs. Railroad sidings surrounded the buildings so the railcars could be unloaded "within easy reach of all departments." There was also enough space between the sidings and the buildings to ensure the company could expand the plant without having to relocate the tracks.[25]

Continued expansion became a core strategy. "In a few years we expect to have three or four times our present capacity, and naturally will have much to offer in the way of advancement," J. O. Eaton predicted.[26]

Viggo Torbensen took pride in the company's deliberate attention to manufacturing processes. "Every one of our 500 or more factory employees today are accomplishing as many operations as several men did in 1912, and system is the reason," he explained. "System in forwarding. System in drilling a number of holes by means of a jig instead of one at a time to an inaccurate punch mark. System in every department—buying, storing, milling, machining, assembling, delivery, and accounting. It is through system and the saving of manual labor—the gaining of a minute here and

# VIGGO V. TORBENSEN

BY THE TIME MACHINIST VIGGO Torbensen met J. O. Eaton in 1911, he had been fine-tuning his internal gear-driven rear axle for more than a decade. His invention was a dramatic improvement over the chain-driven axles common at the time. His axle featured a forged steel I-beam over the driving mechanism, which supported the truck's weight, leaving the driving mechanism free to power the truck while maximizing power, reducing gas and oil usage, and providing less wear and tear.

Born in Copenhagen in 1858, Viggo Torbensen studied at the Royal Danish Naval Academy, then earned a scholarship to study naval and marine engineering in England. After he completed his studies, he worked as a machinist for a year at England's Midway Railway. He immigrated to the United States in 1881, settling in Philadelphia, where he worked as a machinist with machine tool manufacturer William Sellers and Company. After several other jobs of increasing responsibility, he was hired as a supervisor for the Philadelphia subway system.[1]

He also cofounded a steam yacht and launch company named Clay & Torbensen. However, by the 1890s, he had become fascinated by the concept of the experimental "horseless carriage" and sold his interest in the company to study automobile and motorcycle manufacturing in Germany for two years.

When he returned to the United States, Viggo Torbensen found a job supervising the De Dion-Bouton Motorette Company, a French car company that was one of the largest automobile firms in the world at the time. De Dion-Bouton had just opened its first U.S. factory in Brooklyn, New York. Torbensen quickly came to recognize that De Dion-Bouton's automobile chain drive was very inefficient, and he designed and built the first internal gear drive in the United States for the company.[2]

He soon parted ways with the company to concentrate on development of his own axle. In 1901, he founded Torbensen Gear, of Bloomfield, New Jersey. The company manufactured automobiles and gears. Since most of his cars were sold locally and also serviced at his on-site repair shop, he gained valuable experience by seeing firsthand how well the axles worked over time. This experience allowed him to experiment with new designs and perfect his axle manufacturing techniques.[3]

Viggo Torbensen collaborated with J. O. Eaton to found Torbensen Gear & Axle. When J. O. Eaton founded Eaton Axle in 1920, Torbensen joined him at the new company. However, in 1921, Viggo Torbensen left Eaton Axle to start two new companies in Cleveland—the Torbensen Motor Car Company and the VigTor Axle Company.[4] From then until his death in 1947, Torbensen focused his research efforts on refrigeration technology, patenting several important innovations in that field.[5]

a scrap of material there—that workers, employer, and customer benefit alike."[27]

## Generous Employee Benefits

Torbensen Axle placed a great emphasis on providing its employees with generous benefits and a pleasant work environment. "It is the sincere desire of the company that every one of you shall feel that the Torbensen plant is not merely a place to labor for a livelihood, but is also a place where we can really

enjoy our work and associations," wrote factory manager Willard F. Rockwell, an automotive engineer who later founded the Rockwell Corp. "We want the company to assume such a personality that each of us may feel that the concern is our biggest and best friend."[28]

After six months on the job, workers received life insurance. When employees wanted to further their education, Torbensen Axle paid part of their tuition and offered loans to cover the rest.[29]

The company covered hospitalization for work-related injuries and compensation for lost work time. Workers with minor injuries were sent to Miss Hornberger, the full-time nurse at the company's dispensary. "Miss Hornberger will be glad—in fact, it is a special hobby of hers—to go into the homes of any of our workers if their families need any assistance or attention," proclaimed an article in the company newsletter. "This is especially desirable where there are babies and small children. You will find her advice well worthwhile."

Above: The Torbensen plant had a dispensary for treatment of minor injuries. On-duty nurse Miss Hornberger administered first aid, shared wellness advice, and helped develop the cafeteria menus.

Right: Torbensen's company-wide newsletter was launched in 1918 and featured letters from management, news on employee benefits and additions to the plant, and on the company's championship baseball team.

Women also worked on the shop floor. According to the *Torbensen Internal Opinion*, "The number of women we employ is increasing every day, and our facilities are being increased accordingly." These included women's restrooms and locker rooms.[30]

To cut down on hazards, workers were issued safety goggles and respirators. Lubricants and cooling compounds were tested before they were introduced into the workplace. If toxins were found, the company refused to use them.[31] At the time, such concern was far from common practice.

According to the *Torbensen Internal Opinion*, the plant also had a small cooperative store, a recreation hall where "employees are encouraged

*The Torbensen* Internal Opinion

Issued for the employees of The Torbensen Axle Company Cleveland Ohio

NUMBER THREE                    JUNE 1919

to participate in athletic sports of all kinds," and a cafeteria that offered low-cost, nutritious lunches at cost. "Miss Hornberger says that nourishing and wholesome food is essential to the production of good work," proclaimed the newsletter.[32]

The company also made sure employees had plenty of leisure activities, including dances, barbecues, picnics, and organized sports. Workers formed bowling leagues and played tennis in a court at the front of the plant that was open to all employees. Tennis enthusiasts had a standing invitation to try to best J. O. Eaton, an avid tennis player. The baseball team was a particular point of pride, winning Cleveland's all-city championship in 1918.[33]

The annual company picnic at Willoughbeach Park featured a baseball game between the shop and the office, along with a tug-of-war match between the machine shop and the assembly room. Of the tug-of-war, the *Torbensen Internal Opinion* noted: "This contest was surely exciting, but no decision was reached at the picnic, and so it had to be finished out in front of the factory the following Monday." Entertainment included a performance by the company marching band, which favored "patriotic airs." Open to all musically inclined Eaton employees, the Torbensen Band performed at Eaton functions and also gave lunchtime concerts in the shop.

As a result of these employee programs, Torbensen workers remained very loyal and dedicated to the company. According to Markt, "The number of dismissals was small and turnover was at a minimum."[34]

Along with its high regard for its employees, the company in turn had high expectations for their productivity. Torbensen Axle was known for its excellent customer satisfaction and the entire staff remained meticulously devoted to quality in every aspect of the manufacturing process. "One little mistake on someone's part can give 1,000 people a wrong impression of Torbensen axles," J. O. Eaton wrote in a letter to employees, emphasizing the necessity of careful workmanship.[35]

## Wartime Production

As World War I approached, the nation's attention again turned to the need for a better transportation system. According to *A Nation on Wheels*, the rail system simply could not handle the volume of food shipments and supplies earmarked for overseas transport. "Boxcars full of produce, some of it perishable, stacked up along tracks and freight yards, often 50 or 60 miles from major seaports," the author noted.

Inadequate roads led to shipping delays, and lawmakers began to recognize that interstate highways could ease the strain, allowing some of the nation's 325,000 trucks to assume greater responsibility for long-haul shipping.[36]

In 1916, Congress passed the Federal Aid Road Act, allocating $75 million to improve rural roads. State highway departments distributed the funds and provided matching money.[37] The U.S. Council of National Defense's Highway Transport Committee, led by automobile industrialist Roy D. Chapin, sent caravans of military trucks on the first long-distance truck haul, from Detroit to the East Coast.[38]

Inflatable pneumatic tires designed specifically for trucks were a significant innovation introduced during the war. Inflatable tires improved traction, shock absorption, and steering over the solid rubber tires common at the time, allowing trucks to handle heavier loads.[39] These advances led to a skyrocketing expansion of the trucking industry.

The Cleveland-based White Motor Company, which used Torbensen Axle components in its trucks, began manufacturing automobiles at the turn of the century, but during World War I the company became heavily involved in manufacturing military trucks. By the end of the war, truck manufacturing had become such a lucrative business that White stopped making passenger cars altogether and focused solely on trucks.[40] The highway system continued to improve, especially as the U.S. Army freed up surplus trucks to help build roadways throughout the country.[41]

As the trucking industry grew in prominence, so did Torbensen Axle. Sales more than tripled from 1916 to 1917, and the number of rear axles produced increased from 10,068 to 28,484. The company also began making front axles, and introduced axles for 5-ton trucks (in addition to the axles it was already producing for ¾-ton, 1-ton, 2-ton, and 3½-ton trucks). Manufacturing space had increased in one year from 34,000

# A NATION OF TRUCKS

WRITER H. G. WELLS predicted in 1901 that truck fleets would soon eclipse the railroads as a method of carrying cargo cross-country.[1] The eventual growth of the trucking industry proved key to Eaton's early success, although the shift took longer than Wells expected since the country had to first build roads capable of accommodating large vehicles on cross-country trips. Eaton's first product was a two-speed rear axle for trucks that offered extra power under the toughest conditions.

In 1907, Chicago held the nation's first motor truck show. Demand for trucks was promising enough that at least one automobile manufacturing company, Autocar, stopped making automobiles and switched exclusively to 1½-ton trucks.[2] Five years later, Packard built the first truck to cross the country on its own power. A five-man crew of Teamsters made the journey, carrying three tons of Parrot Brand Olive Oil Soap from Philadelphia, Pennsylvania, to Petaluma, California. It took them 91 days of traveling along mostly unpaved roads.[3]

However, it wasn't until World War I that the U.S. had built enough roads to support the long-haul trucking industry. As Mark S. Foster explained in his book *A Nation on Wheels*, during the prewar era, "road-building efforts in the United States were uncoordinated and ... largely ineffective." The general public perceived interstates as frivolous "'peacock alleys' which primarily served wealthy Americans with too much leisure time on their hands."[4]

In 1916, Congress passed the Federal Aid Road Act, allocating $75 million to improve rural roads. State highway departments distributed the funds and provided matching money.[5] The U.S. Council of National Defense's Highway Transport Committee, led by automobile industrialist Roy D. Chapin, sent military trucks on the first long-distance truck caravan, which traveled from Detroit to the East Coast.[6] Pneumatic (inflatable) tires specifically designed for trucks were another important innovation introduced during the war. Inflatable tires offered improved traction, shock absorption, and steering over solid rubber tires, allowing trucks to handle heavier loads.[7]

to 110,500 square feet, and included "greatly enlarged machine shops and stockrooms, a new assembly building, a heat-treating plant, and a powerhouse," along with a new railroad siding and a railroad platform for outgoing freight.[42]

J. O. Eaton was optimistic enough about the future that in 1917 the company spent $100,000— 8 percent of the previous year's sales and 62 percent of profits—on a national campaign to build name recognition. Ads for Torbensen Axle appeared in the *Saturday Evening Post*, *Collier's*, *Life*, and *Scientific American*. As he explained to stockholders, "By this means, our company and our product have attained nationwide publicity, and Torbensen Axles are known and accepted as standard wherever trucks are used."[43]

In Alma, Michigan, Republic Motor Truck Company, Torbensen Axle's largest customer, also prospered during the war as truck orders poured in from the U.S. Army. Four-year-old Republic Motor Truck had tripled its output from 1916 to 1917, selling 12,914 trucks. It was the country's largest exclusive truck manufacturer, and in a few short years would manufacture one out of every nine trucks on the road.[44]

Flush with profits, Republic made an attractive offer to buy Torbensen Axle, its key parts supplier. Torbensen stock was trading high at $92 a share, making it an opportune time to sell. Shareholders approved the sale, receiving a 4-to-1 trade of Republic stock as part of the deal. J. O. Eaton became the first vice president in charge of finance at Republic, while remaining as general manager of Torbensen Axle.

In its Annual Report that year, Republic executives were enthusiastic about the Torbensen

Torbensen Axle customer White Motor Company specialized in trucks early on, and would eventually dominate the truck manufacturing industry. This steam-powered truck was built by White in 1900. *(Photo courtesy of Cleveland Public Library Photograph Collection.)*

By 1920, more than a million trucks were on the road, and Torbensen Axle customer White Motor Company of Cleveland was the industry leader in truck manufacturing. Torbensen Axle's success in the truck market gave the company the capital it needed to diversify, and it soon branched out into automotive parts, and eventually aircraft components. Eaton's truck business remains vital today, especially considering the company's groundbreaking innovations in the field of hybrid truck engines.

The Cleveland-based White Motor Company, which used axles made by Torbensen Axle in its trucks, had been founded as an automaker at the turn of the century, but during World War I, the company became heavily involved in manufacturing military trucks. By war's end, truck making had become such a lucrative industry that White stopped manufacturing passenger cars altogether, focusing solely on trucks.[8] The highway system continued to improve, especially as the U.S. Army freed up surplus trucks to help build roadways.[9]

purchase. After the purchase, Republic was proud that the company would no longer have to depend on an "outside maker" for "this most important factor in the success of the Republic truck."[45]

By 1918, Torbensen's output approached 31,000 axles annually—somewhat short of the 1917 prediction of 40,000 to 50,000 axles, but still higher than all of the other axle manufacturers combined.[46] Many Torbensen products were sold to the military as part of the country's ongoing war efforts. That year, Republic sent 76 trucks with Torbensen axles to Japan. It expected to send 152 more in the following months. "Every completed axle is a solid shot aimed at the heart of autocratic tyranny," proclaimed the *Torbensen Internal Opinion*.[47]

After World War I ended on November 11, 1918, truck production in the United States did not slow down. In fact, the expansion of the trucking industry had only just begun. By 1920, the country could boast 269,000 miles of surfaced roads, with 2 million vehicles being produced annually.

In the next decade, J. O. Eaton would take advantage of the lessons he learned at Torbensen to found Eaton Axle. Under J. O. Eaton's guiding hand, his new company would flourish, experiencing exceptional growth while laying the groundwork for a successful and diversified future.

# EATON AXLES

*The axle shown here — Model 1002, for 1-ton trucks, Model 1502 for 1½-ton trucks — is the silent, spiral bevel gear drive. Rigid cast housing. Double internal brakes, fully enclosed. Straddle pinion mounting. Oversized chrome-molybdenum steel axle shafts mounted on double-thrust bearings.*

THE name EATON on an axle is almost air-tight insurance for the owner against time out for axle repairs. That's the result of Eaton's skilled engineering, scientific selection of materials and painstaking workmanship.

THE EATON AXLE & SPRING COMPANY · CLEVELAND, OHIO

This detailed ad for Eaton Axle appeared in *Automotive Industries* magazine on December 30, 1926.

## CHAPTER TWO

# A LEAP FORWARD
## 1918 – 1929

*Customers wanted cars. Getting cars to the customers was the hard part.*

—*Pioneers, Engineers, and Scoundrels:
The Dawn of the Automobile in America.*[1]

ORLD WAR I ENDED IN NOVEMBER 1918 with the signing of the armistice between the Allied Powers and Germany. By then, Torbensen Axle had already converted its plants to focus on commercial manufacturing. However, many of its customers were still in the process of reconfiguring their factories to once again build civilian vehicles.[2]

Henry Ford had been impatiently waiting for the day when his Ford Motor Co. assembly lines could produce Model Ts again. Mere hours after the armistice was signed, Ford announced that he wanted all tanks removed from his tractor plant so that he could return to building cars. Manufacturers such as Ford and Eaton, which had quickly converted their plants back to commercial use, fared best at the end of the war. The rest were left scrambling when the military work dried up.[3]

Business proved particularly slow in early 1919 as Torbensen Axle waited for carmakers to resume operations. Still, Torbensen executives predicted that things would pick up soon and that the company would have its best year yet. Approximately 70,000 Torbensen truck axles were already on the road, and Oldsmobile had placed an order for 10,000 sets of axles for its

new 3¼-ton light delivery truck that February.[4]

According to the *Torbensen Internal Opinion*, Torbensen Axle had never lost a customer, and in recent years had successfully lured away many new customers from competitors in the United States and abroad.[5] However, Torbensen Axle would soon face an unexpected competitor—cofounder J. O. Eaton. In 1919, Republic Motor Truck stock sold at a high of $53 a share. Torbensen Axle was "reputed to be the largest producer of rear axles in the world," according to the *Cleveland Plain Dealer*, and would see $5 million in revenue and $400,000 in net profits that year.[6]

J. O. Eaton and several colleagues had decided the time was right to sell the company stock they had acquired when Republic purchased Torbensen in 1917. In late 1919, they sold their shares and used the proceeds to form the Eaton Axle Company. The new firm manufactured both conventional axles for passenger cars and new oil-lubricated,

Early Eaton Axle car heaters were installed in the floor of the vehicle.

internal-gear truck axles designed by Viggo Torbensen. "This design makes for maximum delivery of driving power to the rear wheels and overcomes mechanically all of the outstanding objections to truck axles in the past," according to early company brochures.[7]

J. O. Eaton took advantage of the contacts he'd made in the investment banking community to raise $5 million in financing to build Eaton Axle's first factory. In January 1920, the company purchased 16 acres of land on E. 140th Street and the New York Central tracks in Cleveland and began construction of a one-story, 145,000-square-foot plant at a cost of $1 million. The roof featured an innovative zigzag or sawtooth design that conserved heat and maximized natural light.[8]

### A Difficult Market

Automobile manufacturers had high hopes for an economic boom after World War I. However, postwar prosperity was very short-lived due to a combination of inflation, labor issues, and the logistical difficulties of selling cars directly to customers. Strikes by steelworkers, machinists, and axle and bearing makers disrupted production, and the prices for car components soared. Some carmakers simply could not handle the rising prices as they struggled to convert their plants back to commercial production. "Customers wanted cars," wrote Beverly Rae Kimes in *Pioneers, Engineers, and Scoundrels: The Dawn of the Automobile in America*. "Getting cars to the customers was the hard part."

To compensate for higher production costs, car prices rose, in some cases almost doubling. Unfortunately, Americans no longer had the extra funds to support the burgeoning industry. By 1920, they had already cashed in their Liberty War Bonds and spent the proceeds. To make matters worse, credit was not readily available, since the Federal Reserve had tightened borrow-

ing regulations in an effort to slow inflation.[9]

Despite the difficult market, Eaton Axle was able to keep its plants operating continuously during the 1921 recession.[10] However, surviving the downturn proved a difficult task. "We didn't know from one paycheck to another whether we'd be paid or not," recalled Logan Monroe, an accountant who started at Eaton Axle in 1920. "I was afraid of losing my job because there just weren't any [other] jobs to be had. ... The company was a lot better prepared for the Depression of the 1930s when that came along."[11]

### Opportunities During Difficult Times

The recession severely affected Standard Parts, a Cleveland manufacturer of leaf springs (metal braces used in vehicle suspension). The company had $24 million in assets and $26 million in debt. While still a lucrative operation, with the tightening of the credit market, carrying a large amount of debt meant severe cash flow problems.[12]

In search of a solution, Standard Parts stakeholders approached Eaton Axle with a merger proposal. It was a tantalizing proposition. If the deal went through, J. O. Eaton would preside over a $60 million auto parts conglomerate that would be the nation's largest manufacturer of axles, springs, bearings, and rims. The newly formed entity would have a significant edge in the marketplace since the merger would simplify the distribution process for potential clients, who would be able to buy an extensive array of parts from a single company.

The acquisition took place in February 1920. J. O. Eaton became president and general manager of Standard Parts. Under the terms of the deal, he also remained president and general manager of Eaton Axle, which retained its corporate identity.[13] Eaton Axle received 9,000 shares of Standard Parts stock immediately, along with 15,000 additional shares to be held in trust and delivered throughout the next three years.

Logan Monroe, an Eaton Axle accountant, described hard times at the company during the 1921 recession.

The first priority was to increase available cash flow, so J. O. Eaton immediately arranged for long-term financing of $6 million in six-month bank notes and $8 million in five-year, 8 percent notes. He sold 80,000 shares of common stock to pay for the six-month notes, and several banks agreed to invest $6 million in the new stock if stockholders purchased at least $2 million worth of stock.[14]

Standard Parts' stockholders voted to approve the deal, but two court actions complicated the process. Four Standard Parts stockholders filed suit to ban the sale of bank notes. They were unhappy with the stock issued to Eaton Axle, as well as the fact that the new financing plan froze dividends to common shareholders until the bank notes were paid.

Around the same time, Standard Parts supplier Erie Malleable Iron Company of Erie, Pennsylvania, filed a petition to liquidate Standard Parts. According to the petition, Standard Parts only owed Erie Malleable $81,000, but with $6 million in bank notes due in September 1920 and $3 million in other debts, the company stood on the verge of bankruptcy.[15]

The court placed Standard Parts in joint receivership in September 1920, naming as co-receivers J. O. Eaton and Frank A. Scott, vice president of Cleveland-based machine tool manufacturing firm Warner & Swasey. At first, prospects for Standard Parts seemed hopeful. The company was far from insolvent, with $9.5 million in debt but $12 million in current assets and $10 million in fixed assets.[16] However, by 1921, Standard Parts' financial situation had worsened considerably, and the company began to liquidate its assets, including the brand-new Eaton Axle plant on Cleveland's East Side.

# WHY CLEVELAND?

To succeed in the automobile industry, Torbensen Axle needed to be near the center of the automobile industry. By 1914, it looked like either Cleveland or Detroit would be that center. At first, J. O. Eaton was undecided. However, his wife, Edith, felt a strong preference for the city of Cleveland and its older, more established cultural and social scene. According to *The History of Eaton*, "It was clear that New Jersey was never going to be the center of automotive activity. It was also clear that ultimately that center would be in either Cleveland or Detroit. Cleveland newspapers were already calling their city the 'automotive capital.' But while J. O. Eaton was trying to

decide where to place his bet, his wife, Edith, intervened."[1]

As Ford, General Motors, and Cadillac established headquarters in Detroit, however, it became clear that the new hub of the automobile industry would be in Michigan, not Ohio. Cleveland's specialty automobile manufacturers, including Winton and Stearns, had mostly vanished by the 1920s, as the rise of Ford's ubiquitous Model T eclipsed the market for expensive boutique vehicles. The *Encyclopedia of Cleveland History* explained that "the manufacturers and financiers of Detroit were more willing to take the risks involved in building the massive plants required to shift assembly line mass production than were

comparable businessmen in any other manufacturing center of the nation."[2]

Instead, Cleveland became the country's hub for automobile parts and the manufacturing of the assembly line machines that produced cars. Along with its early experiences manufacturing automobiles in the 1900s and 1910s, the city "had ready access to steel, glass, and rubber," noted the *Encyclopedia of Cleveland History*. "It had many companies with experience in using the machine tools necessary to make the equipment for assembly lines, it had large pools of both skilled and unskilled workers, and it was a major transportation center."[3]

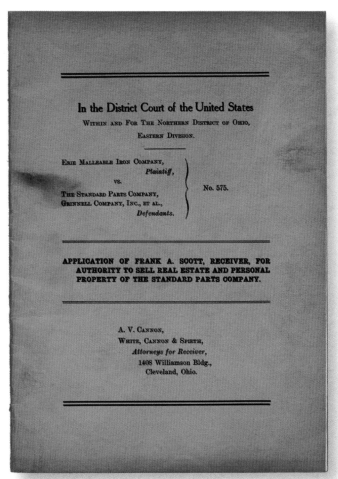

In the District Court of the United States

WITHIN AND FOR THE NORTHERN DISTRICT OF OHIO,

EASTERN DIVISION.

ERIE MALLEABLE IRON COMPANY,
                    Plaintiff,

        VS.

THE STANDARD PARTS COMPANY,                    No. 575.
GRINNELL COMPANY, INC., ET AL.,
                    Defendants.

APPLICATION OF FRANK A. SCOTT, RECEIVER, FOR
AUTHORITY TO SELL REAL ESTATE AND PERSONAL
PROPERTY OF THE STANDARD PARTS COMPANY.

A. V. CANNON,
WHITE, CANNON & SPIETH,
Attorneys for Receiver,
1408 Williamson Bldg.,
Cleveland, Ohio.

Above: This court document from September 1920 asked that co-receiver Frank Scott of Warner & Swasey be given the authority to liquidate the assets of the Standard Parts Company. J. O. Eaton and his investment partners purchased many Standard Parts assets, including the Eaton Axle, Perfection Spring, and Pontiac Spring plants, as well as service stations in Cleveland and New York.

Right: Longtime employees at Torbensen Axle received commemorative pins.

## A Tempting Opportunity

As Standard Parts began liquidation procedures, J. O. Eaton resigned from his receivership position and in 1921 joined Otis and Company, the Cleveland investment banking firm that had helped him finance Eaton Axle. He was well suited to his new job, which involved finding new investment opportunities.[17] A very interesting opportunity

came along in 1922, when J. O. Eaton set his sights on Republic Motor Truck, which had enjoyed great prosperity during World War I as a major producer of "Liberty Trucks" for the Army. However, after the war, Republic's fortunes fell, and by 1921 it was in the middle of a major reorganization.[18]

To raise enough cash to pay off its debts and obtain new financing, Republic attempted to sell Torbensen Axle, J. O. Eaton's former company. Sensing an incredible opportunity, J. O. Eaton decided to buy Torbensen Axle back.

In 1923, as Standard Parts was liquidating its remaining assets to resolve $7 million in debt, J. O. Eaton bought back the Eaton Axle plant at E. 152nd and Nickel Plate in Cleveland for $1.125 million. He also acquired the Perfection Spring plant in Cleveland and the Pontiac Spring plant in Pontiac, Michigan. He took his new company public and orchestrated the sale of 140,000 new shares of stock to raise cash to expand. The new stockholders later approved his proposal to change the company's name to Eaton Axle & Spring.[19]

## Springing into Success

Local power brokers were excited about the new owners of Torbensen Axle. "Eaton and his associates constitute substantially the same group of men who directed the company in the period of its prosperity," noted the *Cleveland Plain Dealer*.[20]

The acquisition of Perfection Spring would also prove extremely advantageous. The company already had a long history in Cleveland, having been formed in 1906 out of a blacksmith shop on the Superior Viaduct, where three men hand-manufactured six to eight chassis leaf springs per day, utilizing high-quality alloy steel imported from the Krupp works in Essen, Germany.[21] Perfection Spring was the first company to manufacture leaf springs specifically for cars—up until that time, suspension springs for cars were essentially the same as buggy springs. The company's profile rose considerably in 1910, when Standard Oil Company mogul John D. Rockefeller brought his car to the Perfection plant to be outfitted with the "newfangled" leaf springs. In 1914, the company built a large plant at Central and E. 65th Street to accommodate rising demand.[22]

Above: J. O. Eaton (center) wears a suit and fedora as he pays a visit to the Eaton Axle & Spring plant.

Below right: This 1923 photograph shows the drilling of Cadillac I-beams at the Eaton Axle plant.

It was an advantageous time for J. O. Eaton to build an auto parts empire in Cleveland. With its proximity to major steel firms, Cleveland was fast becoming a hub for vehicle assembly. The Fisher Body Division of General Motors had just completed construction of a massive plant on Coit Road in Cleveland, not far from the Eaton Axle plant. In 1922, the new plant produced 150 car bodies each day, a number that would quadruple within the next two years.[23]

By 1923, Eaton Axle & Spring had 1,651 customers and was well on its way to surpassing expectations, producing 150,000 axle sets per year and 10,000 springs daily. It had three plants, approximately 5,000 employees, 31.7 acres, and 573,000 square feet of operating space.[24] Eaton Axle & Spring supplied parts to five of the six largest automakers in the country, and 20 of the 40 largest. Its customers for passenger car axles included Cadillac, Pierce-Arrow, Wills Sainte Claire, and Peerless.[25]

Constantly on the lookout for ways to expand, J. O. Eaton foresaw possible opportunities for expansion in a new type of automotive part—the bumper. Early automobiles had no bumpers. In 1920, two brothers in Albany, New York, had developed a new kind of car armor, bending lengths of brass pipe and bolting them to a car's front and

back. They founded the Cox Brass Manufacturing Company and began mass-producing these bumpers, which at the time were sold as aftermarket accessories.[26]

In 1923, Eaton Axle & Spring purchased Cox Brass Manufacturing Company. The timing could not have been better, as an increase in traffic, along with higher driving speeds, required automobile makers to raise their safety standards. In the late 1920s, as bumpers became standard on new cars, Eaton Axle & Spring was well equipped to mass-produce them. After purchasing Cox, Eaton Axle & Spring automated the bumper production process, utilizing new, state-of-the-art machinery.[27] Bumper material changed from brass to nickel-

plated steel and then chromium-plated steel, although Eaton did manufacture a gold-plated bumper for the king of Siam.[28]

Always seeking more efficient ways to run his plants, J. O. Eaton reorganized the layout of the Perfection Spring factory in late 1923, finding enough extra space to also house Cox Brass operations (and equipment including nickel-plating vats and enameling ovens) along with Eaton Axle headquarters.[29] The plant also upgraded its railroad sidings and buildings, and modernized its furnaces and spring manufacturing machinery.[30]

Despite the new acquisitions, Eaton Axle & Spring remained profitable, and by the end of 1923 the company had completely paid off its debts.[31]

## Partnership with Ford

In 1920, an inventor in Bellingham, Washington, Charles E. Starr, patented a two-speed axle with a planetary differential that gave the car a lower low gear, a higher high gear, and two reverse gears, making it more adaptable on hills and treacherous road conditions. Seeing potential in this innovation, businessman and race car enthusiast Glover E. Ruckstell worked out a deal with Starr and the Ford Motor Company to use the axles on its Model T cars and trucks. The axle "really made a difference in the performance of the Model T, greatly increasing its climbing ability and pulling power."[32]

By 1925, 200,000 Ruckstell axles were already on the road. Production for 1926 was expected to jump to around 100,000 axles.[33] Unfortunately, the Ruckstell Sales and Manufacturing Company did not have the capacity to match the demand for the popular axles.

Starr, who still owned the rights to the patent, offered Eaton Axle & Spring a license to produce his axles for Ford passenger cars and trucks in exchange for royalties. By 1926, "Eaton was vigorously advertising the new axle concept and business was brisk."[34]

Demand proved even higher than expected, and in just two years, Eaton Axle & Spring produced

This ad for Eaton bumpers appeared in the *Chilton Automobile Directory* in the late 1920s.

Eaton began manufacturing Ruckstell axles for Ford Model Ts in 1926.

500,000 Model T axles. When Ford discontinued the Model T in 1927, Eaton engineers adapted the Ruckstell axle to heavy trucks.[35]

## New Acquisitions, New Opportunities

Even as he found success in new business deals, J. O. Eaton continued searching for new opportunities to expand. In November 1925, Eaton Axle acquired the American Auto Parts Company of Detroit, makers of chassis leaf springs and a subsidiary of American Steel Foundries. The plant's location was very attractive to J. O. Eaton, who hoped to establish facilities in Michigan, a fast-growing hub for the country's major automobile makers. After the acquisition, a new corporation was formed called the Eaton Spring Corporation, with all common stock owned by Eaton Axle & Spring and all preferred stock owned by American Steel Foundries.[36] Many production duties were moved to the new Detroit facilities, and the spring plant at Central Avenue and E. 65th Street in Cleveland was converted to the manufacture of bumpers.[37]

In 1926, Eaton Axle & Spring secured its spot as the largest manufacturer of automobile springs in the country after purchasing the Beans Spring Company of Massillon, Ohio. President John F. Beans was named the president and general manager of the new Eaton Spring Corporation. The largest customers of the combined company included Cadillac, Studebaker, Packard, Ford, and the General Motors Truck Company.[38]

After the acquisition, Eaton began purchasing 10,000 to 12,000 tons of steel monthly—about half of the entire steel bar production of the United Alloy Steel Corporation. Due to the costs associated with the acquisition, Eaton Spring Corporation showed a loss that year, but J. O. Eaton was optimistic that "progress had been made during the past year in rounding out the organization and plant facilities, and Eaton Spring now had the opportunity to demonstrate its earning power."[39]

After deciding to spend the majority of his time at Otis and Company, the Cleveland-based investment firm where he served as a partner, on September 11, 1924, J. O. Eaton announced he would be stepping down as president of Eaton Axle & Spring to serve as the company's chairman of the board. He was succeeded by C. I. Ochs, a close associate who had been vice president and general manager of Eaton's Axle Division. Ochs managed the company's day-to-day operations.[40]

To raise cash, in 1927, Eaton Axle & Spring sold the old Torbensen plant, which it no longer used for manufacturing, and which had been leased to another firm for years. Following the sale of the plant, Eaton Axle & Spring acquired all of Eaton Spring Corporation's preferred stock from American Steel Foundries, gaining total control over all of Eaton Spring and its subsidiaries.[41]

## A Decade of Growth

After dominating the spring market, Eaton Spring branched out into the burgeoning automotive heater and gas cap manufacturing fields. In February 1928, Eaton Spring acquired Perfection Heater & Manufacturing Company of Cleveland.[42] Founded in 1909, Perfection Heater produced the first automotive heater in 1914. Its early heaters were a gas exhaust type, installed in the car floor. Next came heaters that were made by steel-jacketing the manifold. In 1925, Perfection pioneered hot water recirculation heaters, and by 1928, the company had sold more automobile heaters than any other company in the world.[43]

In July 1928, Eaton Spring purchased the Easy-On Cap Company, which manufactured gas, radiator, and crankshaft caps. The Easy-On Cap Company was founded in a small fabricating plant in the back of a filling station on Cleveland's East

# GROWTH OF AN AMERICAN COMPANY

IN THE BEGINNING, EATON WAS strictly an American company focused on vehicle components manufacturing. Early on, the company's founder, J. O. Eaton, wisely decided to move operations from Bloomfield, New Jersey, to Cleveland, Ohio. The new location placed Eaton closer to its customers and suppliers— Detroit automobile manufacturers, and the steel plants that supplied the necessary raw materials.

After a few false starts, the truck axle business proved very lucrative during World War I, when the U.S. highway system began to improve and the country's cargo transport system began the shift from freight trains to trucks. However, J. O. Eaton was dedicated to diversifying the company beyond axles. An astute businessman with a knack for sizing up promising companies, he believed from the beginning that the best

way for Eaton to grow was through acquisition. In 1919, he deftly orchestrated a merger between Eaton Axle and the Standard Parts Company. Although nearly as large a company as Eaton Axle, Standard Parts was overextended and needed a lifeline. J. O. Eaton arranged for a consortium of Cleveland

bankers to invest $25 million in the merger. He also retained the Eaton Axle name and led the newly merged company as president and general manager.

While Standard Parts eventually failed, J. O. Eaton wisely purchased Torbensen Axle, and then acquired many of Standard Parts' facilities as

Eaton workers attach tie-rods and bolt steering components to front axles.

Side.[44] Its founders patented a simple but necessary object—a threadless, one-quarter-turn cap used for gas tanks, radiators, and crankshafts. Easy-On Cap Company pioneered the use of a locking cap mechanism that offered tremendous improvements over the unwieldy conventional screw-top caps of the time.[45] Easy-On later introduced a hubcap for wire wheels that by 1928 was used in all but three of the most popular automobiles manufactured in the United States.[46]

The acquisition of Easy-On Cap marked the beginning of Eaton's Stamping Division. Eaton built a new cap production plant next door to its axle

plant at E. 140th Street. Within a year, the plant was producing more than a million caps per month.[47] Eaton also acquired a plant from Cleveland vehicle-parts manufacturer Monmouth Products Company, adding to its cap-producing capacity.[48]

In 1928, Eaton brought in $1.5 million in profits, and the dividend was increased from $2 to a "gratifying" $3 per share, according to the company's Annual Report that year. "We are looking forward to a very satisfactory business for the current year."

A story in the *Cleveland Press* marveled at Eaton Axle & Spring's ability to sustain a high part of the company's liquidation procedures. Eaton Axle & Spring was reborn from the ashes, stronger than ever.

The acquisitions continued at a fast pace throughout the 1920s, as Eaton added bumpers, gas caps, hubcaps, and automobile heaters to its product lines. Profits grew from $195,000 in 1924 to $1.5 million in 1929. Growth was strategic but conservative. When the Depression hit, Eaton was healthy enough to survive, while continuing to acquire innovative companies such as Wilcox-Rich in 1930, which successfully manufactured valves, tappets, and lifters, but lacked liquidity during a period of economic hardship.

J. O. Eaton recognized great potential in one particular Wilcox-Rich product—the sodium-cooled valve, a heavy-duty engine valve that could withstand higher temperatures than conventional valves. At the time of the acquisition, sodium-cooled valves were just beginning to gain success as valuable components in aircraft engine production.

The Wilcox–Rich acquisition paid off by the late 1930s, with Europe facing the start of World War II in 1939. As car production halted, factories converted to wartime production, and the demand for sodium-cooled valves for military aircraft increased exponentially. Combined with the production of truck axles for wartime use, manufacturing valves kept the company very busy.

Eaton emerged from the war in good shape and ready to invest more money in research. J. O. Eaton recognized that it would take more than acquisitions to provide the company with cutting-edge technology. Eaton needed its own team of innovative engineers to develop new products and improve existing product lines. In 1948, the company broke ground on a new research complex in Southfield, Michigan. The facility brought together engineers who worked on a variety of components, allowing them to better coordinate projects while collaborating in a central location.

In 1958, Eaton acquired Fuller Manufacturing Company of Kalamazoo, Michigan, and its subsidiary, Shuler Axle Company. Fuller was the largest producer of heavy-duty truck transmissions, and Shuler was a major supplier of trailer axles, truck front steering axles, and air brakes.[1] This important acquisition gave Eaton the opportunity to offer full medium- and heavy-duty transmissions alongside axles, springs, and other Components, and solidified its position as a leader in the industry.

By the late 1950s, Eaton would begin growing internationally, establishing subsidiaries in Europe and South America to manufacture components for those markets. It was the beginning of a global focus that would one day bring Eaton products to more than 150 countries. However, the company would owe much of its international success to the solid foundation Eaton had built by manufacturing vehicle components for the U.S. marketplace.

---

manufacturing capacity of 6,000 axles per month at its E. 140th Street plant. By then, Eaton Axle & Spring was manufacturing components for five of the six largest truck producers in the nation, and "practically all" school bus manufacturers. Next door at the stamping plant, "huge presses stamp out the metal caps with precision and rapidity. To protect workers' hands from the jaws of these presses into which they feed metal sheets, straps, affixed to the wrist and timed perfectly with the press operation, pull the hand back automatically as the jaw of the press descends."[49]

In four years, Eaton Axle & Spring's profits increased more than sevenfold, from $195,000 in 1924 to $1.5 million by the end of 1928. A year later, as the Great Depression descended on the nation, Eaton's profits, beginning in September 1929, fell to $450,000, "due to the sharp decline of activities in the automotive industry," according to the 1930 Annual Report.[50]

Despite the uncertain economic climate, the diversified company that J. O. Eaton had carefully engineered was built to withstand the difficult times to come.

As this service brochure shows, Wilcox-Rich continued to make valve lifters after Eaton acquired the company in 1930.

## CHAPTER THREE

# BEYOND THE AXLE

## 1929–1939

*The Grapes of Wrath, that saga of the Depression, showed some of the poorest Americans moving westward across the desert in old automobiles—but in automobiles nevertheless.*

—Mark S. Foster, *A Nation on Wheels*[1]

THE AUTOMOBILE INDUSTRY ENJOYED an unprecedented surge in business in 1929. That year, 5 million cars were produced for an American public accustomed to easy credit and plentiful, well-paying jobs.[2] "The automobile industry was never in a more favorable condition than it is at the present time," wrote Detroit analyst Fred Kingsbury in June 1929. "Production and sales during the last four months have reached new high levels and, while there has been a slight tapering off in output at a few plants, the majority of the manufacturers report large numbers of orders on hand."

Although small-town bankers were tightening up their lending policies, automakers showed little concern that the lack of readily available loans would hurt their industry.[3] However, the Black Tuesday stock market crash of October 29, 1929, marked the start of the Great Depression, which sent the U.S. economy plummeting. By 1930, auto production had dropped 30 percent from the year before, to 3.5 million cars. President Herbert Hoover tried to give the numbers a positive spin: "We have been cheerful in the use of our automobiles," he told a gathering of auto industry executives. "I do not assume they are being used for transportation to the poorhouse. While I am aware that many people are using the old automobile a little longer, it is obvious that they are still using it and that it is being worn out."[4]

Despite the president's predictions, by July 1930, demand for cars had plummeted, and Chrysler cut the pay of its salaried employees by 10 percent and reduced the hours of its wage earners.[5] Since auto manufacturers had previously been overly optimistic about long-term demand for cars, dealers across the country were burdened with excessive inventories of unsold cars, further decreasing demand.[6]

However, unlike his fellow manufacturers, J. O. Eaton saw the economic downturn as an opportunity to complete some important acquisitions. Just before the crash, the board had raised a substantial amount of cash by increasing capital stock from

This advertisement promoting Eaton's Lubri-Flex springs appeared on the back cover of the *Eaton Eye* newsletter. First published in 1939, the *Eaton Eye* featured news about Eaton managers and suppliers.

Before it became part of Wilcox-Rich and, later, Eaton, Rich Steel had its own baseball team.

300,000 to 1 million shares, a fortunate decision that gave the company the funds necessary to invest in its diversification efforts.[7]

At the time, J. O. Eaton had been focusing his efforts on Otis and Company, the investment banking company where he was a partner. C. I. Ochs, Eaton's new president and general manager, essentially ran Eaton Axle & Spring. Unfortunately, Otis and Company lost a fortune during the crash, which in turn led to a substantial decrease in J. O. Eaton's own personal wealth. He decided to cut his losses and part ways with Otis, which by 1931 had shuttered its investment and brokerage business. Instead, he wisely shifted his focus to strengthening Eaton Axle & Spring. Although he had lost much in the Black Tuesday crash, he remained financially stable, maintaining residences in Cleveland Heights, Ohio, and Williamstown, Massachusetts. Still, his fiscal sit-

uation forced him to begin drawing a $36,000 salary from Eaton for the first time.[8]

## Diversification

In February 1930, Eaton acquired Detroit-based Peterson Spring Company, which specialized in coil springs such as valve, brake, die, and lock springs. Customers included Cadillac, Chevrolet, Chrysler, Ford, Packard, and Peerless. This acquisition further diversified Eaton's important Spring Division, which had previously only manufactured leaf springs.[9]

That same month, J. O. Eaton began the process of acquiring Wilcox-Rich Corporation, of Saginaw, Michigan, which manufactured valves, tappets, and lifters.[10] Founded in 1913 as Wilcox-McKim, Wilcox-Rich originally manufactured automobile steering gears and outboard motors. It became Wilcox Motor and Manufacturing Company in 1916 after Milton Wilcox acquired full ownership of the company. During World War I, the company produced boosters and adapters for shells. After the war, the company was renamed Wilcox Motor Parts and Manufacturing Company, specializing in manufacturing automotive valves, then merged with aircraft valve manufacturer Rich Steel Products of Battle Creek, Michigan, to become Wilcox-Rich.[11]

At the time of the transaction, Rich Steel was a leader in the production of heavy-duty, sodium-cooled aircraft valves that could withstand higher temperatures than conventional valves. Sodium-cooled valves were invented by U.S. Army Air Corps engineer S. D. Heron, who discovered that valves heat-treated with salt would absorb heat. Rich Steel researchers worked with Heron to develop a commercially viable salt-cooled valve capable of handling temperatures 275 to 300 degrees higher than untreated valves. Charles Lindbergh's *Spirit of St. Louis* was one of the first planes to use sodium-cooled valves. Soon, all engines above 300 horsepower in commercial and military aircraft utilized sodium-cooled valves.[12]

By 1929, Wilcox-Rich had opened several new facilities in Michigan, including a tappet plant in Marshall, a valve plant in Battle Creek, and a Saginaw plant making valve lifters, valve seat inserts, and satellite-faced rings. Its facilities and equipment were state-of-the-art, but the company lacked liquidity.[13] According to the *New York Times*, the combined assets of Eaton and Wilcox-Rich at the time of the acquisition were $19 million, making Eaton one of the largest automotive parts manufacturers in the United States at the time. Combined net earnings for 1929 were $19 million.[14]

After the acquisition, Eaton announced that its research team would be led by Robert Jardine, who had previously led the sodium-cooled valve research efforts as chief engineer at Wilcox-Rich. Under Jardine's leadership, Eaton engineers developed valves containing metallic sodium that melted at lower temperatures than other sodium-cooled valves. As the metallic sodium melted, the valve began to remove heat as soon as the engine began to warm, dispersing heat more efficiently than traditional sodium valves. This important development allowed manufacturers to build larger aircraft engines. Eaton also developed lighter leaf springs made of grooved steel and pioneered a technique known as "shot pelleting," a manufacturing technique designed to increase the life of its leaf springs by bombarding them with steel pellets.[15]

In the Wilcox-Rich transaction, Eaton acquired stock in Erb-Joyce Foundry Company, a Wilcox-Rich subsidiary based in Vassar, Michigan. Founded in 1920, Erb-Joyce specialized in manufacturing cast iron for use in engine blocks, pump housings, and valve bodies.[16] The foundry's name was changed to Eaton-Erb Foundry, and it later

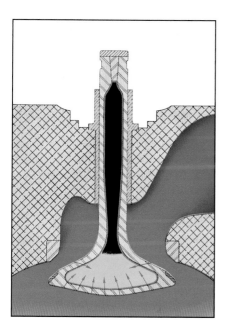

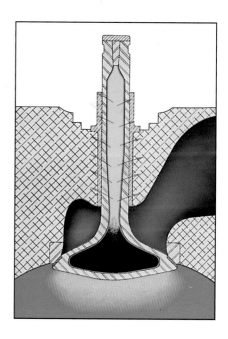

The success of Eaton's sodium-cooled valves, invented by U.S. Army Air Corps civilian engineer S. D. Heron, helped keep Eaton's production lines running during the Depression. Heron discovered that valves heat-treated with sodium would absorb heat. Rich Steel researchers worked with Heron to develop a commercially viable salt-cooled valve. During the manufacture of a sodium-cooled valve, pure sodium is inserted into a cavity in the head and stem (above). During normal operation of an internal combustion engine, the valve head absorbs heat from the combustion of gases (left). The liquid sodium absorbs the heat and is thrown into the stem, transferring the heat to the valve guide, then to the cylinder and cooling system (right). Eaton's sodium-cooled valves could withstand temperatures of up to 1900 degrees Fahrenheit, 275 to 300 degrees higher than untreated valves.

Eaton's Foundry Division in Vassar, Michigan, made permanent mold gray iron castings, which were sold to manufacturers specializing in refrigerators, cars, washing machines, typewriters, electric irons, pistons, tractors, and carburetors.

became the site of operations for Holley Permanent Mold Machine and Holley Carburetor Company of Detroit, another Eaton acquisition during that time period.[17]

## Resiliency in Hard Times

From 1930 to 1931, the output of cars in the United States fell from 3.5 million to 2.4 million. Because of the steep decline in auto manufacturing, Eaton's profits dropped from $1.2 million in 1930 to $243,471 in 1931.[18]

Despite the downturn, Eaton acquired several companies that year, including Reliance Manufacturing Company of Massillon, Ohio, which manufactured 50 percent of the lock washers in the United States. The Reliance plant had the capacity to make up to 3 billion lock washers each year.

The 20-year-old company, founded by local entrepreneur Frank C. McClain, had warehouses in New York and Detroit. Its main plant in Massillon was located near Eaton's chassis

spring plant. According to the *Chicago Journal of Commerce*, Reliance was a healthy company that earned record profits in 1929.[19] It had consistently grown until 1930, when its net earnings dropped by 58 percent, from $536,000 in 1929 to $226,000.[20]

In an attempt to cut expenses, Eaton halted its acquisition strategy in 1932. That March, after completing its string of mergers and acquisitions, Eaton Axle & Spring changed its name to Eaton Manufacturing Company to better reflect its diversified operations.[21]

Unfortunately, 1932 was one of the darkest years of the Depression, as 5,000 U.S. banks crashed and 32,000 commercial businesses failed, including most of the smaller carmakers. Consulting statistician Ray B. Prescott had predicted the consolidation of the automotive industry two years earlier, with demand for luxury cars in free fall and smaller companies unable to profitably produce low-cost models. "In the next three or four years, I look for the formation of three or four great corporations as big as any we have in the industry now that, together, will control practically the entire output in this country," he explained.[22]

The Detroit metropolitan area was among the hardest hit by the steep declines, with unemployment at nearly 50 percent by 1932 and near-bankrupt car manufacturers unable to pay their employees. More than 200,000 autoworkers lost their jobs, and those still employed could only find intermittent work.[23]

With the new-car market down a million units from 1931's already-dismal showing, the Ford Motor Company decided to halt production of its popular Model A, the industry's top seller since its introduction in 1927. By August 1931, sales of the Model A "were running at rates only half those of 1930," noted T. H. Watkins in his book *The Great Depression: America in the 1930s.* This occurred despite price cuts in Ford cars that year, and cuts in workers' pay from $7 an hour to $4 an hour.[24]

The downturn in car production—and demand for car parts—took its toll on Eaton. "Production reached such a low point in 1932 that the utmost economy in cost and expenses could not be sufficient to avoid a substantial loss," J. O. Eaton wrote in the company's 1932 Annual Report.[25]

Facing the looming prospect of insolvency, Eaton was forced to institute layoffs and reduce hours and wages for all of its remaining employees. According to J. O. Eaton, despite the difficult circumstances, the substantial pay cuts "have been accepted in a splendid spirit of loyalty and cooperation."[26]

In the first quarter of 1933, Eaton lost a record $237,000. However, in March 1933, President Franklin Delano Roosevelt took office, and in June 1933, Congress passed the National Industrial Recovery Act, which earmarked funds for welfare-relief projects and public works, including building new roads. New jobs and thousands of miles of new highways could only help the industry, predicted Charles H. Larson, president of the Automobile Merchants Association of New York. With traffic congestion an increasing problem in metropolitan areas, and some cross-country rural roads still primitive, "where will the city, the county, the state, and the nation get the roads and highways on which the automobiles, the trucks, and the buses are to travel?" he added. "That is the problem which is worrying the leading automobile merchants as much as the sales factor."[27]

Cars bought during the prosperous 1920s were beginning to wear out beyond the possibility of repairs. Yet, despite the precarious economic climate, Americans were not willing to give up their automobiles. "Whatever the hardships and painful experiences of Americans during the Depression years, they did not give up their auto-

In 1930, Eaton added coil springs to the production lines at its Detroit spring plant, which was already manufacturing leaf springs.

# HELPING OUT EMPLOYEES DURING HARD TIMES

J. O. EATON ALWAYS THOUGHT that being a responsible employer involved more than just handing out paychecks. His philosophy was that well-treated employees were loyal employees, and loyal employees rewarded the company by doing good work. To foster that loyalty, he continually looked out for the welfare of his workers' families by providing life and health insurance long before such benefits were standard. He hired a full-time nurse to promote wellness and treat workplace injuries. She even made occasional home visits to families with newborn babies. J. O. Eaton also established Eaton's first of many company cafeterias in 1919, which provided nutritious meals at a low cost. He also ensured employees had plenty of social and recreational opportunities, including baseball leagues, picnics, and a tennis club.

Eaton even had a company marching band that played in the factory at lunchtime.

Unfortunately, during the Great Depression, Eaton was forced to reduce employees' hours and cut their pay to ensure the company's survival. J. O. Eaton tried to institute the new policies as humanely as possible, keeping as many men on the payroll as he could, even if it meant giving them only one or two days of work a week, recalled former Eaton accountant Logan Monroe. "About two-thirds of our employees had some income, but at times that was not enough to cover their grocery bill," Monroe recalled.

One afternoon, J. O. Eaton walked into Monroe's office and asked what they could do to help workers pay for basic necessities. Monroe talked to the company's welfare office and representatives from the City of Cleveland to find out

the minimum amount of money needed to support a family of one to 10 people. J. O. Eaton then took out a $300,000 loan to provide extra help for his struggling employees.

"We told our men that we wanted them to always have food in their house," said Monroe. Each payday, they cut each worker a separate check—usually around $2.50—to reconcile the difference in their payroll checks. "It was considered a loan (without interest) and could be paid whenever they felt their income had recovered enough for them to get along without direct company help," he explained.[1]

Future Eaton CEO Sandy Cutler considered Eaton's ethical behavior one of the unique strengths that has always helped the company stand out from its competitors. "Long before it became stylish, Eaton was founded on a belief and commitment to doing business right," Cutler said. "The values ... of individual employee participation, recognition, employee safety, and treating people with dignity and respect are a culture which began long ago."[2]

Workers gather for a group photo at one of Eaton's early plants.

mobiles, probably because they did not have to," wrote historian John Lukacs. "[During the 1920s,] the number of private automobiles in the United States dropped less than 10 percent. By 1935, their number reached the level of 1929 and grew thereafter every year."[28]

A firm supporter of President Roosevelt, J. O. Eaton was optimistic and felt certain that the economy had begun to turn around. By mid-1933, he raised workers' salaries between 30 to 35 percent and began hiring new employees. By the end of the year, Eaton had recouped its losses, with profits surging to $360,000.[29]

New policies also helped stabilize the auto industry. At the president's urging, most automakers adopted the Automobile Code that designated a minimum wage for auto industry workers and a maximum number of hours per week employees could work. The cap on hours was intended to give each employee "a reasonable amount of work per year," according to the code, and spread out automobile production throughout the year, thus avoiding the typical plant shutdowns common during the winter months. The code also gave employees the right to organize labor unions without risking their jobs.[30]

Roosevelt asked car manufacturers to move the annual New York Automobile Show from January to November, to help create more buzz and, ostensibly, more demand for automobiles in the winter. The change was long in coming. As early as 1929, Chrysler analyst John W. Scoville had complained about the bad timing of the show, and encouraged a reduction in auto prices throughout the winter, alongside an increase in summer, to cut down on seasonal fluctuation, which he considered "an evil of long standing."[31]

According to R. H. Grant, then vice president of sales at General Motors, the public needed a push to change its buying habits. Consumers tended to purchase cars in the summer months, perhaps due to the early days of the automobile, when roads were generally treacherous and cars had no heaters and canvas tops.[32]

The industry embraced the idea. According to the *New York Times*, "It is expected that the November show will result not only in spreading employment more evenly throughout the year in the automobile industry, but also in doing the same for

This 1938 photo shows the interior of Eaton's Cleveland axle plant.

the steel industry and suppliers of parts and materials for automobiles."[33]

As car sales crept upward, Eaton began moving forward with new acquisitions. Following a September 1933 merger with Detroit Metal Specialties, Eaton formed a new subsidiary corporation called Eaton–Detroit Metal Specialty Corporation that manufactured small stampings, hubcaps, stove fittings, and automobile trunks. Eaton originally intended to consolidate its resources by improving operations efficiency in the company's underperforming Easy-On Cap Division. The main facilities for Eaton–Detroit Metal Specialty Corporation were in Detroit, with additional bumper plants in Cleveland. Under the merger, Eaton added several new products to its inventory, including hubcaps and vertical bumper guards. However, the plan was not as successful as the company anticipated, and by 1936, Eaton had moved the subsidiary's bumper operations from Detroit to Massillon, Ohio, only to dissolve the subsidiary in 1938 and transfer its Massillon bumper operations to Cleveland.[34]

Eaton also began streamlining its bumper operations, which were split between a plant in Cleveland, Ohio, and a Jackson, Michigan, plant that Eaton acquired in the 1934 purchase of Alloy Spring & Bumper Company. Eaton shut down its Cleveland bumper plant and consolidated its bumper operations in Jackson, reconditioning and expanding the facilities for maximum efficiency. "Bumpers are a highly competitive field and even slight differences in cost are the difference between profit or no profit," J. O. Eaton explained. "Inasmuch as we could make bumpers slightly cheaper in Jackson ... we decided to make bumpers there."

Jackson also had the advantage of slightly lower wages than Cleveland, he added, mentioning Cleveland's unwillingness to protect plant property during strikes and the "too liberal attitude of newspapers during acute labor difficulties."[35]

## Union Politics

Cleveland was a hotbed of union activity after the newly formed United Auto Workers (UAW) began organizing in the area in 1934. Over the next seven years, all of Eaton's automotive parts plants would gradually be unionized.[36]

Eaton's bumper plant in Jackson, Michigan, had 102,000 square feet of floor space and was located on 34 acres.

Local 45 of the Coit Road Fisher Body plant in Cleveland, an Eaton neighbor, became a major site of UAW activity. In 1937, it was the site of the first major union sit-down strike, a strategy that would soon become a major UAW organizing tactic. After two union organizers were demoted, a shift of 135 workers sat down inside the plant. A few days later, in solidarity with their Cleveland peers, thousands of UAW members in Flint, Michigan, shut down the Fisher Body plant with a sit-down, seizing property and forcing security police to leave the premises.

According to historian T. H. Watkins, the Flint workers "had seized not merely a couple of the physical plants of an automobile company, they had taken hold of hope itself, and before it was over, their exploit would reverberate with greater force than any other single act of organized labor in the years of the Great Depression."[37]

Strikers slept on unfinished automobile seats and fought police with makeshift weapons fashioned from car roof beams and door hinges. Their families and friends slipped food through the plant windows and confronted police and security workers in the streets.[38]

Cleveland UAW workers then faked a sit-down at Chevrolet plant No. 9. Police showed up only to find that the real strike was happening at Chevrolet plant No. 4.[39]

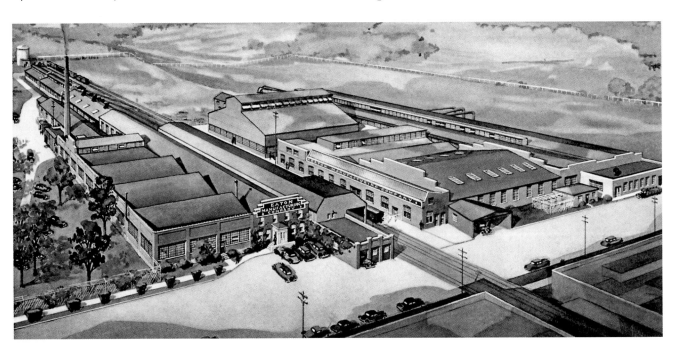

After 44 days of sit-downs, General Motors faced daunting production losses—from 15,000 cars weekly in January 1937, down to 151 cars weekly in the first 10 days of February.[40] On February 11, 1937, the company signed a one-page document guaranteeing the UAW the right to unionize its workers.[41]

By the end of 1937, sit-down strikes had successfully created 256 local unions and 400 union contracts in the automobile industry. The UAW had 375,000 members. Historian Michael Smith noted that unions were particularly successful during the Depression—although jobs were scarce and theoretically car companies could easily replace rebellious workers—because conditions were especially terrible and workers felt they couldn't question their treatment.[42]

Above: Clarence Cross' union card was typical of those issued to Eaton workers beginning in the 1930s. He was a member of the United Auto Workers (UAW).

### "Eaton's Outlook Bright"

Eaton more than held its own during the mid-1930s, with its profits rising slowly but steadily as the auto industry recovered. "Depression is a forgotten word in the automobile industry, which is forging ahead in production, retail sales, and expansion of productive capacity in a manner reminiscent of the '20s," proclaimed a 1936 article in *BusinessWeek*.[43]

By 1934, Eaton was gaining a healthy profit of $1.1 million, triple that of the previous year. It had 11 plants and more than 5,000 employees and was well positioned to make more acquisitions.[44] The company bought out the remaining interests in its Vassar, Michigan, foundry, to create its Foundry Division in 1935, which produced castings for the equipment in its plants. Along with sand mold castings, Eaton began manufacturing less-costly permanent mold castings.[45] Eaton also acquired a valve plant in Detroit that year, purchasing the net assets of the Detroit Motor Valve Company to increase its valve-making capacity.[46]

In 1936, Eaton announced profits in excess of $1.8 million, a record not surpassed since the start of the Great Depression in 1929. A story in the *New York Times* that year, headlined "Eaton's Outlook Bright," described an "optimistic" J. O. Eaton sailing for Coventry, England, to open a new aircraft com-

Left: Clarence Cross became an Eaton Manufacturing employee in 1932 after the Wilcox-Rich acquisition. This is a typical Eaton employee I.D. badge from that era.

ponents plant. In the article, Eaton predicted 4.25 million to 4.5 million automobiles and trucks in production that year.

A reporter for the *New York Times* wrote a story describing 1936 as "a great junking year," meaning that the wave of people who hadn't bought a car since the stock market crash could no longer repair their aging vehicles. Cars "used beyond their normal expectation of life throughout the Depression years" were expected to head for the scrap heap, replaced with new models.[47]

Car manufacturers agreed that moving the date of the auto show, along with implementing the Automobile Code, helped keep an additional 150,000 autoworkers employed through the winter. Automotive and allied industries' payrolls tripled from 1933 to 1936.[48] By 1932, the auto industry's products, including parts, had a wholesale value of $793 million. In 1936, that figure rose to $3.6 billion.[49]

Eaton finalized three acquisitions that year, buying out minority shareholders in Eaton-Erb Foundry and Eaton–Detroit Metal, and purchasing the remaining assets of Wilcox-Rich. The company also completed construction on its research and engineering facilities in Detroit.[50]

## A Bump in the Road

By the end of 1937, the U.S. economy had taken a turn for the worse. With the grim memories of the early years of the Depression still fresh in their minds, consumers were saving more, leading to a decline in consumer spending and a backup of inventory reminiscent of the late 1920s. Out of $9 billion in national wages in 1936, $3 billion went into the bank. Unsold goods were valued at $5 billion in mid-1937.[51]

President Roosevelt's job cuts in the federally funded Works Progress Administration (WPA)—the largest New Deal program, providing government

Eaton's heater plant in Cleveland manufactured aftermarket car heaters as well as factory-approved heaters installed in new cars. The new-car heaters brought year-round business to the heater plant, which previously had shutdowns when demand was low in the warmer months.

jobs in road building, the arts, literacy, and public works—handed another blow to the economy. In an effort to reduce federal spending and work toward a balanced budget, Roosevelt slashed WPA employment from 3.7 million to 1.9 million. Although jobs in the private sector were up 4.7 million, the sudden loss in federal jobs struck fear in consumers already worried about a repeat of the 1929 crash. According to historian T. H. Watkins, these factors cumulatively produced "an economic crisis whose emotional impact was reminiscent of that from the crash of 1929, precisely because recovery, on the face of it, had appeared to be proceeding slowly but steadily."[52]

On October 19, 1937, the stock market dropped 75 points, down to 115. It would continue to slide until May 1938, losing two-thirds of the value it had gained. Four million jobs were lost in March 1938 alone, increasing unemployment to 20 percent.

Car sales plunged, as did Eaton's profits. "Your company is feeling the effects of the general depression, especially in the automobile industry," wrote J. O. Eaton in a letter to stockholders at the end of 1937. "The results of operations in the first quarter of 1938 will not be favorable."[53]

In 1938, Eaton's sales dropped 41 percent from the previous year, and the company lost $589,164

With war looming and the demand for sodium-cooled valves for aircraft on the rise, the Wilcox-Rich Division's Battle Creek, Michigan, plant underwent its third expansion in two years by 1939.

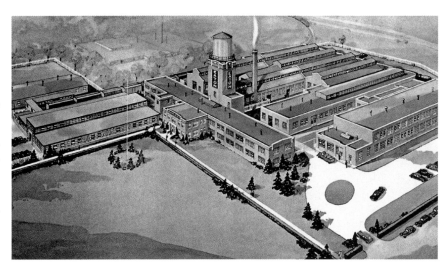

in the first nine months. However, after Roosevelt authorized $3.75 billion in new federal spending, the economy began to improve considerably. In the last three months of 1938, Eaton's sales had nearly returned to 1937 levels.[54]

The Heater Division, which produced heaters for new cars, greatly increased its volume. And sales of sodium-cooled aircraft valves rose 75 percent. Valve orders came from Mitsui of Japan at first—37,750 by October 1939. However, as the world chose sides and geared up for the start of World War II, their orders ceased, replaced with orders from France and Wright Aeronautical Corporation in the United States.[55] With the prospect of war looming, Eaton built an addition to its Battle Creek plant to manufacture sodium-cooled valves.[56]

By 1938, Eaton was supplying valves to 34 of the nation's 51 aircraft manufacturers.[57] Its automotive divisions were also prospering, with a huge jump in sales of cars and trucks in the first quarter of the year. The *New York Times* noted the health of the auto parts industry, with 36 parts makers reporting aggregate net profits of $13.2 million—compared with a net loss of $2.2 million in the first quarter of 1939. Eaton's profits jumped from $200,000 to $725,000 in three months.[58]

Eaton now had eight divisions, all of them profitable—Axle, Spring, Bumper, Spring Washer, Stamping, Valve and Tappet, Heater, and Foundry. In Cleveland, the company had plans to increase its E. 140th Street axle plant by one-third. At its E. 65th and Central plant, it had just finished remodeling and retrofitting to manufacture water

heaters for several carmakers as well as the replacement market.[59]

Additionally, Eaton was fortuitously situated at the crossroads of the truck manufacturing industry. Industry leader White Motor Company, maker of White trucks, was located near Eaton's axle plant, as was Euclid Road Machinery Company, which manufactured off-road trucks and construction vehicles. Nearly 50 industrial laboratories in the city developed and tested parts and materials, including engine blocks and cylinders, shock absorbers, and heat-resistant steel for engine valves.[60]

Eaton's two-speed truck axles, which allowed drivers to choose from twice as many high and low gears as standard axles, quickly became the industry standard. Gears on every vehicle went through two rounds of tests at the factory to make sure they could withstand the stress and strain of heavy-duty use. "A truck so equipped has eight speeds and a wide range of gear ratios for power, speed, and economy," noted the *Cleveland Press*. "This special rear axle gives an owner two trucks in one, insofar as pulling power, speed, and economy are concerned."[61]

By the end of the decade, Eaton had survived the worst. According to J. O. Eaton, "The year 1940 finds us with a large amount of business booked, and we see no reason why the results should not prove satisfactory to our shareholders."[62]

Beginning in 1940, the United States required all men between the ages of 18 and 45 to register for the draft. By the end of World War II, 3,069 Eaton employees had served in the armed forces.

## CHAPTER FOUR

# SURVIVING AND THRIVING
## 1940 – 1949

*There is hardly an auto, truck, or aircraft made in America which does not have some part manufactured by various divisions of the Eaton Manufacturing Company or its subsidiaries.*

—*Cleveland Plain Dealer* [1]

OUR PRESIDENT IN HIS PROGRAM FOR THE DEFENSE OF AMERICA

THE UNITED STATES OFFICIALLY entered World War II after the bombing of Pearl Harbor on December 7, 1941. However, by 1940, the U.S. had already begun preparing for war as the Axis powers invaded Europe, China, and the Soviet Union. President Franklin Delano Roosevelt's first weapons-making priority was the production of state-of-the-art warplanes. Calling on the U.S. automobile industry to build 50,000 aircraft by the end of 1940, he set up the Office of Production Management to supervise the conversion of existing plants from civilian to wartime production and to make provisions for constructing additional factories. [2]

In 1940, Eaton began converting its plants for wartime production, as had most U.S. automobile manufacturers. That year, mainly because of defense obligations, Eaton substantially increased production, floor space, and equipment at its Battle Creek plant (aircraft engine valves), Saginaw plant (tappets, seat rings, and miscellaneous aircraft parts), and Cleveland axle plant (axles for military trucks and aircraft engine parts). [3]

At the Battle Creek plant, aircraft engine valve output tripled from 1939 to 1940. To keep up with demand, Eaton expanded the forge and heat treatment departments and added equipment and a manufacturing wing. The British government furnished additional equipment to produce 24,000 pieces per month of Packard Rolls-Royce aircraft engine valves. This production doubled in 1941, and a second addition was built. From its original plant space of 9.4 acres, the Battle Creek operation expanded to more than 25 acres by 1943. [4]

The Cleveland expansion included the construction of a new building dedicated solely to the manufacture of aircraft engine parts. Defense work also began at the Marshall valve plant, the Detroit spring plant, the Cleveland stamping and heater plants, and the Massillon spring washer and wire plants.

While Eaton initially covered the substantial expenses required to convert its plants for military production, by the end of 1940, the company began negotiating leases with the Defense

---

Anticipating America's eventual involvement in World War II, President Franklin Delano Roosevelt authorized the creation of the Office of Production Management in 1940 to supervise the conversion of existing manufacturing plants from civilian to wartime production.

EVERY HOUR AND 20 MINUTES SOMEBODY MAKES A PLANT SUGGESTION! HOW ABOUT YOU?

Above figure is based on single shift 40-hr., week.

During the early 1940s, plant efficiency was critical to the war effort. This editorial cartoon from the *Eaton News* encouraged workers to offer suggestions on ways to boost production, cut costs, and increase safety.

## Union Clashes

In early 1941, a union conflict that made national headlines idled several Eaton plants. During this time, both the American Federation of Labor (AFL) and the Congress of Industrial Organizations (CIO) represented different groups of autoworkers. Plant workers in Saginaw were split in their loyalties between the AFL and the CIO.

Eaton's Saginaw plant shut down after violence broke out between striking CIO workers and non-striking AFL workers who attempted to cross the picket line. State police intervened, using tear gas in an attempt to disperse the crowd, but five officers and two workers were injured in the incident.

CIO workers in four other Eaton plants went on strike in solidarity with the Saginaw workers, shutting down those plants as well. According to the *New York Times*, tensions surrounding the work stoppage grew over the next three days until a federal mediator ordered everyone back on the job as "an urgent matter of national defense."[7]

As 1941 progressed, so did Eaton's war output. In Eaton's Battle Creek plant, aircraft engine valve production doubled again. By December, the plant had 2,047 employees, up from 335 employees three years before.[8] In addition, Eaton's Detroit Spring Division rose from two to three shifts and hired 150 additional employees, many of them women, to meet increased demand.[9]

## Ready for War

On December 7, 1941, 353 Japanese aircraft descended on the U.S. Naval Base in Pearl Harbor, Hawaii, launching a surprise attack that killed 2,402 Americans. The following day, President Roosevelt delivered his famous "Day of Infamy" speech, and Congress declared war on Japan. By mid-December, the United States had fully entered into World War II, following Germany's declaration of war against the United States.

Plant Corporation, a government agency established to stockpile weapons materials and subsidize the wartime industry.[5] From 1941 to 1943, the Defense Plant Corporation built $26.8 million worth of new plants for Eaton.

As the company switched from peacetime manufacturing to wartime production, Eaton simultaneously built components for military vehicles and for passenger cars for the general consumer. Eaton also began manufacturing components for two of the earliest automatic transmissions available—the fully automatic Hydra-Matic Drive for Cadillac and the semi-automatic Fluid Drive for Chrysler.[6]

Days after the bombing, J. O. Eaton designated the Cleveland stamping plant on E. 140th Street as a research facility for war machines. During the war, the facility engineered improvements in tank ventilators, thermoelectric generators, and the manufacture of axial-flow jet engine compressor blades.[10]

War production ramped up in 1942; by February, all automobile companies had halted production of consumer goods. A month later, the production of civilian trucks ceased, although military truck production would quadruple by 1944.[11]

During the war, Eaton's manufacturing space doubled from 30 acres to 60 acres, and its workforce jumped from 3,600 to 18,000 employees. The company produced $500 million in war material, out of $29 billion produced by the automobile industry overall.

Eaton supplied parts for Chrysler's tanks, Ford's armored combat vehicles, Pontiac's antiaircraft guns, Studebaker's Jeeps, and General Motors' machine guns. The Axle Division made two-speed axles for all types of weather, ranging from conditions in Alaska, to those in the Sahara, Europe, the South Pacific, and Russia. During the course of the war, the Stamping Division produced more than 200 million detonators and millions of gas tank caps for military planes.

In Michigan, Eaton's Battle Creek plant manufactured sodium-cooled valves for warplanes such as the B-17 Flying Fortress, the B-25 Mitchell Bomber, and the P-47 Thunderbolt. The valve plant in Marshall also produced a heavy-duty hydraulic pump for combat vehicles. Developed by Eaton engineers in 1940, it was widely adopted for military vehicles. It was such a success that in 1941 pump production nearly eclipsed valve production in Marshall.[12]

Weighing in at 52 pounds each, just 12 volute springs could support the entire weight of a 28-ton medium tank.

## Eaton-Made Volute Springs Used For Suspension On Army Tanks

By W. H. WALLACE
Vice President and Manager of Spring Division

Since most military vehicles lacked heaters, the Heater Division in Cleveland converted to manufacturing armor-piercing bullets and aircraft parts. At the Reliance plant in Massillon, Ohio, the Spring Division increased its workforce, from 600 employees prior to the war to 850 by 1943. The plant added a third shift and operated 24 hours a day for 352 days straight. For Eaton's efforts, it was awarded the Army–Navy "E" for excellence.[13]

Under the War Profits Control Act of 1944, companies engaged in war production were required to return "excessive" profits to the U.S. government. A government board determined the appropriate profitability on a case-by-case basis. Due to the War Profits Control Act, Eaton's earnings decreased from $4.4 million in 1941 to $3.7 million in 1944, despite strong sales that more than doubled from 1941 to 1944.[14]

## A Wartime Workforce

Beginning in 1940, all men between the ages of 18 and 45 were required to register for the draft. By the end of 1942, 1,559 Eaton workers were in the service, and thus on leave. By the end of the war, 3,069 employees had served in the military.

Though many Eaton employees went off to war, the company faced ever-increasing production demands. To meet the U.S. government's demand for airplane parts, Eaton expanded its Valve Division to a new plant in a converted winery in Lawton, Michigan, about 40 miles from Battle Creek.

With many of Eaton's male employees drafted into military service, by December 1942, women made up 10 percent of the workforce in the Valve

Division. They worked in most areas of the plant, with the only exceptions being the forge shop, heat treatment area, and tool rooms. Many became skilled machine operators. At its peak in 1943, the Valve Division had 6,200 employees—triple the prewar number. By this time, about a third of those employees were women.[15]

As men and women began working more closely alongside one another in the shop, Eaton made several key institutional changes. In the Valve Division, Eaton established an industrial relations department to handle human resources and personnel issues. That department included a Female Relations Division, staffed by a "matron" and 10 counselors who served as ombuds for the women on staff.

Counselors instructed new female hires on company policies and safety regulations and gave them tours of the infirmary, women's locker rooms, and the lounge, as well as introducing them to their foremen. When necessary, they also helped with finding child care and housing, and with family

Above: In recognition for its efforts in wartime production, Eaton was awarded the coveted Army–Navy "E" for excellence.

Right: With many of Eaton's male employees drafted into military service, women made up an ever-increasing percentage of Eaton's workforce. At its peak in 1943, Eaton's Valve Division had 6,200 employees, and about a third of those were women.

issues. To build camaraderie between new and long-time employees, some plants also established recreation departments, which organized victory garden contests and ping-pong tournaments.[16]

By early 1942, Congress implemented tire and gasoline rationing. That March, Leon Henderson, head of the U.S. Office of Price Administration, told the nation's 30 million car owners that "they were now running on their last sets of tires for possibly three years, and thus had better make them last as best they could."[17]

Rubber was reserved for military vehicle tires. Henderson told the Senate that the situation was so dire "that it might become necessary to commandeer tires from 'family' cars to keep essential vehicles going."[18]

Calling fast drivers "slackers" who "impaired their tires," Henderson also successfully pushed for a national speed limit of 35 mph, which took effect in September 1942. Gasoline rationing was instituted in an effort to compel Americans to cut back drastically on driving to preserve their tire treads.[19]

To build camaraderie between new and longtime employees, some Eaton plants established recreation departments. These departments were tasked with organizing diverse events such as victory garden contests, ping-pong tournaments, variety shows (above), and band concerts (below).

## Hearse Used In Battle Creek Share-The-Ride Plan

We have in the person of Homer Yeckley (right end of the line) of our Battle Creek plant the World's champion Share-The-Rider—and the accompanying photo to prove it. Yes, Homer went out and bought a ten-year old hearse and is now daily driving twelve of his fellow-workers to and from our Battle Creek plant—thus making four tires do the work of fifty-two. Eleven very much alive war workers ride in the body of the hearse (surrounded by plush) and the other rides more conventionally by Homer's side. That totals thirteen —but after all, these men couldn't be superstitious!

Left: To cope with war rationing, employees participated in car-share programs. Here, an article from the November–December 1942 edition of the *Eaton News* highlights how Homer Yeckley of the Battle Creek plant used a 10-year-old hearse to transport 12 of his fellow employees on a daily basis.

Below: Most Eaton plants converted to wartime valve production during the 1940s.

Motorists were limited to gasoline purchases sufficient to fuel about 2,880 miles of driving per year. Workers needing to drive further for occupational purposes could receive a supplement that allowed them 470 miles total per month.[20]

In response to the rations, Eaton plants established car-share programs, where designated drivers received the higher fuel rations. In Eaton's Battle Creek plant, security workers provided a courtesy tire change service in the parking lot for drivers with worn-out tire treads.[21]

With most manufacturing materials scarce, Eaton instituted a salvage plan at its plants. At the axle plant in Cleveland, reconditioned tools were sorted in "rows and rows of orderly bins," according to an *Eaton News* article from the era. Workers salvaged corrugated paper, oil, gloves, cotton items, scrap metals, cutting tools, drills, safety equipment, and electric motors. The program was so successful that it continued after the war.[22]

Eaton and other manufacturers often experienced shortages of raw materials, especially metals such as copper and steel, which were rationed to war contractors through a government program called the Controlled Materials Plan. In 1943, Eaton, Ford,

# A SONG AWAY FROM HOME

IN 1944, ASPIRING COMPOSER AND Eaton axle service department employee Jim Ballantyne penned the tune "They Are Eaton Boys Wherever They May Be." The song was intended to inspire and commemorate Eaton employees serving during World War II.

Eaton published the sheet music in a red, white, and blue cover, then sent a copy to every employee in the military. "It will be played in every corner of the globe," proclaimed the *Eaton News* in July 1944, "lifting the spirits of our own fighting men, telling them we are not forgetting." Much of the newsletter that year was devoted to correspondence between soldiers overseas and their Eaton coworkers back home.[1]

**They Are Eaton Boys Wherever They May Be**

*Some Eaton boys
    are in the Air Corps,
Some are in the
    fighting Marines
Other boys have gone
    with the Infantry
Or the Navy,
    that fighting machine.*

*They are Eaton Boys
    wherever they may be
In the air, on the land
    or at sea;
Gallant and strong
    they go steadily on
For that road leads
    to Victory!
Every Eaton boy is a hero,
No matter where
    he may be;
Let us do our part together
While they're fighting
    for you and for me.*

*Where boys of Eaton
    are now fighting
They won't be so lonesome
    while there,
For in planes and trucks
    and artillery
Eaton products
    are doing their share.*

Studebaker, and many other contractors signed a letter of complaint stating that inefficiencies in the Controlled Materials Plan were making it impossible for them to meet the production deadlines for the Department of War. The letter stated that almost all of the 256 plants surveyed in 27 states, Eaton's included, had not received necessary allotments of materials.[23]

## Peacetime Transitions

By the time World War II ended on September 2, 1945, 64 Eaton employees had been killed and 146 were wounded while serving their country. E. Mandell de Windt, a young personnel clerk and future Eaton CEO, developed a successful plan to ensure that Eaton's returning veterans had jobs waiting for them.[24] However, soon after the war, some of the new workers hired during the war were laid off due to decreased production. At Eaton's Battle Creek plant, for example, the workforce decreased from 5,000 in 1944 to 625 in 1945.[25]

Companies across the country soon began the difficult transition from wartime production to commercial manufacturing. Demand for cars, and thus car parts, was high, since Americans had been deprived of buying new vehicles for four years. However, Eaton still leased much of its increased floor space from the government. Gradually, the company began purchasing those leased plants outright.

In July 1945, Eaton purchased its previously leased Massillon plant from the Reconstruction Finance Corporation, the independent government

Eaton acquired the Dynamatic Corporation of Kenosha, Wisconsin, in 1946. The January 1947 edition of the *Eaton News* celebrates the acquisition.

Featuring DYNAMATIC CORPORATION, KENOSHA
January, 1947

**EATON**
MANUFACTURING COMPANY

PLANTS: Cleveland • Detroit • Saginaw • Marshall • Battle Creek • Lawton • Vassar • Massillon • Kenosha • Windsor (Canada)

agency that had invested in the construction of new plants during the war. At the time, Eaton continued manufacturing the bullet-core steel rods the company had specialized in during the war. Yet, according to the *New York Times*, Eaton remained "in a position to convert immediately to peacetime production."[26]

Eaton also purchased its leased plants in Battle Creek and Saginaw, investing approximately $13.5 million in plant expansion and new equipment in 1945 and 1946. According to the company's 1945 Annual Report, these investments were intended to strengthen Eaton's competitive position "and lead to a larger peacetime volume."[27]

According to economist Joseph Finkelstein, wartime production helped manufacturers such as Eaton prepare to meet the pent-up consumer demand of the postwar economy. To produce large volumes at the lowest possible cost during the war, such companies had spent massive sums on expanding and streamlining their assembly lines. They had improved their management structure, purchased government-owned plants at a fraction of their costs, and taken advantage of generous wartime tax credits that continued long after the war ended. As Finkelstein explained, "Dominant in the field before the war, they would emerge as leaders again."[28]

## The Dynamatic Acquisition

Eaton was in a healthy position to acquire companies that would build on its core strengths and further diversify its products. Its first postwar acquisition was the Dynamatic Corporation, a leading electromagnetic drive manufacturer, in 1946. This marked Eaton's first major acquisition in the electrical field, which would eventually become the largest growth area for the business.

"The Dynamatic Corporation gives [Eaton] entirely new fields for magnetic control of clutches, brakes, dynamometers, machine tools, and oil well equipment," noted Eaton's 1946 Annual Report.

"The automobile industry offers great possibilities, and applications have already been made by one of the largest car manufacturers."[29]

Dynamatic was originally founded in a small laboratory in Kenosha, Wisconsin, in 1931, with just four employees, including brothers and inventors Martin and Anthony Winther.[30] It developed the first eddy current drive, a rotor assembly of magnets and coil fitted into a drum of soft iron.[31] Previously, other companies had tried and failed to make a commercially viable drive. Dynamatic was the first to succeed, soon winning a contract to provide the Pullman Company with 6,900 drives for the air-conditioning compressors in their railcars.[32] Orders from General Motors, Chrysler, Ford, and Westinghouse quickly followed.[33]

In 1936, Dynamatic introduced eddy current dynamometers, heavy-duty engine power testers used in developing high-speed aircraft engines. Three years later, the company came out with

Ajusto-Spede, an adjustable industrial speed drive that combined the drive motor and clutch in the same assembly.

From 1941 to 1946, Dynamatic was involved solely in war production, mostly manufacturing dynamometers for testing aircraft engines.[34] By the time the war ended, Dynamatic desperately needed to expand so the company could keep up with increasing demand. Eaton provided the capital, acquiring Dynamatic as a subsidiary and building a large plant in Kenosha. In 1953, Eaton dissolved the subsidiary and integrated Dynamatic as a full-fledged division.[35]

According to Charles Hickox, a relative of J. O. Eaton, "[J. O. Eaton] was always pleased in getting the Dynamatic Division because he not only got a good line of products, but he also got two geniuses—one of whom became vice president of engineering and the other an inventor who stayed on working on the basis of a trust agreement, the best bargain imaginable."[36]

Right: This photo shows the 24,000-square-foot Dynamatic site expansion under construction in the 1940s.

Below: Eaton's acquisition provided Dynamatic with the necessary capital to conduct much-needed expansion. This 1947 drawing shows the plans for the new plant in Kenosha, Wisconsin.

## Developing the Eaton Brand

Postwar prosperity was in full swing by 1947 as Eaton's profits doubled from the previous year.[37] Optimistic about the market's potential in the near future, Eaton announced its biggest advertising campaign yet. The company spent $500,000 to promote its products in more than 70 business publications.[38] *Tide*, a trade magazine

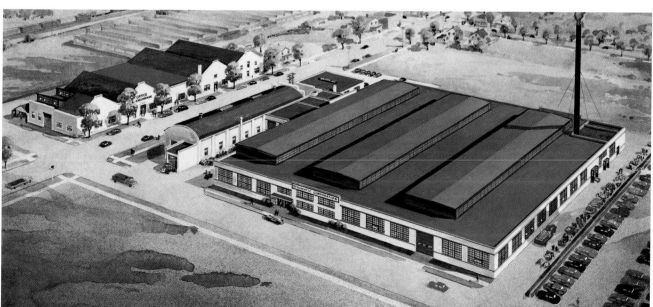

covering the advertising industry at the time, noted that for the first time in more than 20 years, Eaton began running ads for its two-speed truck axles. A new car heater and a thermostatically controlled car engine were also prominently featured in the campaign.[39] The purpose of the campaign, according to the *Eaton News*, was to "make the name 'Eaton' recognized throughout the industrial world, as insurance for when the business situation might not look as promising."

In February 1948, *BusinessWeek* ran a lengthy article detailing the effect of Eaton's Dynamatic Drive. "Eaton started out [trying to] develop a drive to help automakers run accessories," the magazine stated. "It ended up with a device that is edging into wire drawing, home appliances, home heating, textiles, and other fields."[40] The popular Dynamatic Drive was initially used as a power-saving device that turned on the cooling fan in a car engine only when the engine reached a certain temperature, unlike conventional fans at the time, which ran perpetually anytime the engine was turned on. However, the adaptable drive was soon used in windshield wipers, water pumps, and in-home furnaces, thanks to its ability to evenly distribute heat rather than producing heat in surges.[41]

Above: In an attempt to establish a strong position in the postwar world, Eaton ran a series of ads in publications, including *BusinessWeek*, *FORTUNE®*, and *Automotive News*. Combined, these periodicals boasted a circulation of 350,000.

Right: Eaton ratcheted up its magazine advertising after the war, placing ads in some 80 business publications, including this advertisement from 1947 promoting two-speed truck axles.

Eaton's trade campaign proved so successful that Eaton decided to place ads in national general interest magazines, including *Time*, *Newsweek*, and the *Saturday Evening Post*. According to the *Eaton News*, in an effort to reach a broader audience, "a new type of copy with universal appeal was developed which has as its central theme the story of the cross-country truck industry."[42]

During the war, Eaton researchers had fine-tuned several promising innovations, including a rotor pump for trucks and tractors that was adapted for use in combat vehicle transmissions, differentials, and transfer case units. After the war, the

In this 1948 photo, Clyde Garrett, an employee of the Axle Division in Cleveland, operates a new machine called an American Broach. It cut the internal teeth of the ring gear used in two-speed axles.

pump was used in automobiles for operating convertible tops and window operating mechanisms, as well as in automatic transmissions. By March 1948, 100,000 rotor pumps were being produced each month at Eaton's Marshall, Michigan, plant. Eaton's rotor pumps proved so popular that the Marshall plant's valve operations were moved to Saginaw, allowing workers at the plant to focus on pump manufacturing.[43]

Eaton engineers also began work on the first commercially viable power steering pump, along with some innovations in valve durability and truck axles, and the Heater Division began producing a fresh-air heating, ventilating, and defrosting system for cars and trucks. According to a promotional brochure mailed to shareholders, the heating system offered "a complete change of air once a minute [and was] thermostatically controlled to provide comfort and clear vision under all weather conditions."[44]

With a continued emphasis on research, Eaton also announced plans for a new Central Research facility in South Euclid, Ohio, a suburb 15 miles east of Cleveland. Automotive research facilities remained in Detroit, while additional product research continued in individual divisions.[45]

Meanwhile, Dynamatic continued its pursuit of the perfect clutch. Its Magnefluid clutch was powered by millions of fine metal particles suspended in oil that came into contact with a magnetic field. Engineers developed a special seal to keep the metal particles from leaking into the bearings.[46]

Eaton consistently improved its efficiency and operating procedures, placing a high emphasis on customer input. As customers began demanding newer, higher quality cast iron for engine products produced in the company's Saginaw plant, Eaton built a new on-site foundry to allow for better control of the characteristics of the iron and the ability to make minute changes. In addition, the foundry allowed the company to conduct new research and to explore the relatively recent advances in alloy and hardenable irons.[47]

### Farewell to a Founder

In July 1948, J. O. Eaton celebrated his 75th birthday with a large family gathering at his summer home in Williamstown, Massachusetts. Unfortunately, the Williamstown gathering was one of the last times J. O. Eaton would join with his extended family, where "often there were as many as 19 grandchildren falling into the swimming pool on hot, lazy afternoons," recalled Winsor French, one of J. O. Eaton's eight children and the society columnist for the *Cleveland Press.*

The *Cleveland Plain Dealer* mentioned his birthday, noting that J. O. Eaton had been the driving force behind the company's expansion from a small shop in 1911 to 12 plants in 1948.[48] He was also an avid art collector and philanthropist, founding an art museum at his alma mater, Williams College, where he would ultimately bequeath a large portion of his estate.

The *Cleveland News* praised J. O. Eaton for building his reputation on being "a keen judge of men," one who "selected wisely in choosing his branch managers."

The company J. O. Eaton founded also had something to celebrate, as 1948 marked Eaton's 25th anniversary as a public company. That November, Eaton's board of directors approved the company's very first two-for-one stock split.

JOSEPH ORIEL EATON
1873        1949
FOUNDER OF THIS COMPANY

This memorial dedicated to Eaton founder J. O. Eaton was placed in Eaton's Cleveland headquarters a few months after his death in May 1949.

# REMEMBERING THE FALLEN

IN JULY 1949, TWO MONTHS AFTER J. O. Eaton's death, the company dedicated seven sculptures honoring Eaton employees who perished in World War II. As a way of paying tribute to Eaton's veterans, J. O. Eaton had commissioned sculptor and World War II veteran Marshall M. Fredericks to design bronze and granite memorials. Fredericks is perhaps best known for his *Cleveland War Memorial: Fountain of Eternal Life*, which took 19 years to complete.[1]

The Eaton memorials featured a pair of eagles, one in flight and one with wings raised, carrying a plaque that read: "In honor of the men of

this organization who gave their lives for their country," along with the names of the fallen Eaton soldiers. Before his death, J. O. Eaton planned a memorial ceremony unveiling the sculptures. Broadcast simultaneously on an inter-factory network, it featured a Gold Star Mother in each city

placing a wreath on the memorial.[2]

Over time, some of the monuments have been relocated or placed in storage. Eaton is currently in the process of locating the monuments, restoring them, and, in some cases, finding new locations for them. The Saginaw monument, for example, was moved to the Marshall M. Fredericks Sculpture Museum at Saginaw Valley State University after the Saginaw plant was torn down in 2008.[3]

This bronze eagle is featured on the eight Marshall Fredericks sculptures placed in Eaton plants to honor World War II veterans.

---

Unfortunately, J. O. Eaton died of a heart ailment in his Cleveland Heights, Ohio, home on May 15, 1949, at the age of 75. His obituary appeared in numerous papers throughout the Midwest, and nationally in the *New York Times*.

The *Cleveland News* highlighted his wartime contributions, eulogizing that this "mild-mannered man of restless energy and executive drive" had played "a vital part in the successful prosecution of

the last war and in the transportation development of this country."[49]

According to his obituary in the *Cleveland Plain Dealer*, "Cleveland's title of parts supplier [to] the world is in large part a tribute to Joseph O. Eaton. There is hardly an auto, truck, or aircraft made in America which does not have some part manufactured by various divisions of the Eaton Manufacturing Company or its subsidiaries."[50]

# What can <u>I</u> do?

## *You can do <u>this</u>:*

***Understand*** that when your country rallied with the United Nations to halt aggression in Korea, it was notice to the Kremlin that the free nations were not going to be pushed around any more . . .

***Realize*** that the U. S. drive to build our defenses gives us all a new responsibility to make our free American system work even better than it ever has before . . .

***Appreciate*** that the true source of our material strength is the ability of our free people to *produce more* for every hour we work than any other nation—to do it by management and labor *working together* with constantly improved machines, power and skills . . .

***Resolve*** that especially now *you* will do your level best to keep productivity going up. Only in this way can we maintain our high living standards at home, and at the same time produce whatever is needed to stop aggression when and where it comes.

If every one of us does this through the uncertain days ahead we can face the future with confidence.

A PUBLIC SERVICE PROJECT · THE ADVERTISING COUNCIL

## THE BETTER WE PRODUCE . . .
## THE STRONGER WE GROW

As the country geared up for war, the company newsletter *Eaton News* featured ads promoting worker productivity and support for the troops.

## CHAPTER FIVE

# A NEW ERA
## 1950 – 1960

*We like to work on parts that are hard to make. It's a challenge to our engineers and designers, and it gives us a fine sense of accomplishment.*

—H. J. McGinn, Eaton chairman and president, 1956[1]

AT THE START OF THE 1950s, THE U.S. automobile industry reached an all-time production high of 8 million vehicles.[2] General Motors (GM), Ford, and Chrysler had invested heavily in opening manufacturing plants in the Cleveland area. This proved beneficial for Eaton, due to its proximity to the new automotive plants.

GM opened a new, expansive automatic transmission plant for Chevrolet in Parma, a suburb near Cleveland. In addition, Ford Motor Company built a foundry and an engine plant in the area. By 1953, most of Ford's six-cylinder engines and all of its V-8 Mercury engines were being produced in Brook Park, Ohio, a Cleveland suburb. Enjoying record sales, Eaton had its plants running on all cylinders to meet a backlog of orders for its products.

To keep up with the increased demand for its products, Eaton quickly expanded production capacity. By 1950, Eaton had a total of 2.65 million square feet of plant space. Its product lines included automotive gear, aircraft, railroad equipment, farm implements, household appliances, marine and diesel engines, and well-drilling accessories.

However, the early momentum at the start of the decade didn't last, as the U.S. soon became embroiled in the Korean War. During the war, the U.S. government instituted the Controlled Materials Plan (CMP), allowing the Department of Defense to implement price controls and production limits. With no way to know how much steel, copper, and nickel would be set aside for military use, car manufacturers remained uncertain about the amount of raw materials that would be available for commercial production.

In response to these production difficulties, Eaton came up with creative solutions, including purchasing foreign steel, converting unused scrap steel into useable forms, and appealing to vehicle manufacturers for assistance in cutting through government red tape. "In many instances, our customers gave us valuable assistance in procuring or providing materials," noted Eaton's 1951 Annual Report. "Credit is also due to our division managers as well as our entire staff for

---

H. J. McGinn, a former Reliance executive who served as vice president of sales when Eaton bought Reliance in 1930, was Eaton's president from 1951 to 1956 and served as chairman in 1956.

Eaton doubled the size of its Battle Creek, Michigan, plant in order to produce compressor blades for aircraft such as the Boeing B-47 Stratojet bomber. *(Photo courtesy U.S. Air Force.)*

producing a record volume of product under trying conditions."[3]

With plenty of capital at its disposal after several years of prosperity, Eaton began to institute significant equipment upgrades that would allow the company to substantially expand production capacity.[4] In 1951, Eaton announced plans to double the size of its Battle Creek, Michigan, plant to meet demand for its turbojet engine compressor blades.[5] The Battle Creek plant manufactured blades for Lockheed's F-80 Shooting Star and F-94 Starfire, Boeing's B-47 Stratojet bomber, and Grumman's F9F Panther, among many others.[6]

With assistance from the government, Eaton purchased former Air Force buildings at the Battle Creek airport that had previously been used for repairing planes, converting the facility into a forging plant for jet engine blade production. Eaton also fired up its idle valve plant in Lawton, Michigan, for war duty.

"In spite of the many difficulties caused by material shortages, all Eaton divisions are producing and shipping at record rates," noted a letter from management in the July 1951 *Eaton News*. "Even when the war ended, production was expected to remain high."[7]

To keep pace with demand, Eaton announced a $1 million expansion in Marshall, Michigan, that included adding 375,000 square feet to the existing plant. The government helped Eaton expand, contributing $200,000 in equipment for the manufacture of pumps for defense purposes.[8] Further additions were made to the Dynamatic facility in Kenosha, Wisconsin, which obtained a new lab for electrical and eddy current research, and the Reliance Division, which had just completed its most prosperous year and needed more space for the annealing and production of high-quality, cold-finished steel.

As Eaton expanded, the process of acquiring necessary production parts from subcontractors in different parts of the country became more complicated and expensive. To streamline the process, Eaton began manufacturing component parts in-house. In 1952, the company invested $8 million in a new facility for manufacturing automotive parts and forgings. Marion, Ohio, a city of 35,000 approximately 100 miles southwest of Cleveland, was selected as the site for its "proximity to raw materials and to Eaton customers in Michigan, Indiana, and Ohio," as noted in the *Eaton News* in June 1952. With four major railroads serving Marion, as well as its own airport, the city proved ideal for distribution purposes.[9]

A steel strike delayed construction on the 170,000-square-foot plant, but by 1953, the plant was complete. It featured a forge shop, a machine and die shop, and a heat-treating department—along with the latest in glare-resistant paint and lighting to prevent worker eyestrain.[10] Plant workers manufactured air brake components and gears, pinions, and axle shafts for the truck industry. The parts ranged from 3 pounds to more than 100 pounds.[11]

To accommodate new automatic nickel-chrome plating machinery for the automobile industry, in 1954 the company moved its Stamping Division to a plant Eaton had acquired in Cleveland. The new location had 40 percent more manufacturing space than the old plant.[12]

## Innovation Leads to Success

During the Korean War, Eaton had continued to finance its research endeavors. The end of the Korean War signaled the end of the Controlled Materials Plan, which had limited the amount of resources available for commercial production. Once commercial car production resumed at normal levels, Eaton was ready to release several

As part of Eaton's expansion efforts, the Dynamatic Division added a lab for electrical and eddy current research in 1951. *(Photo by Kucera & Associates.)*

### Eaton and the Truck Industry Grew Up Together

Power to pull out of tough spots, to negotiate severe grades under heavy load; speed to maintain fast schedules on the open highway—this is the dual performance which Eaton 2-speed axles give to modern commercial vehicles. Developed more than a quarter century ago by this company, the Eaton 2-speed axle is today used by every major industry.

Among other Eaton contributions to the efficiency and service life of modern trucks and buses are such developments as sodium-cooled valves, hydraulic valve lifters, shot-pelted springs, rotor pumps, and Dynamatic drives.

Through close cooperation with vehicle and engine manufacturers Eaton research and production ingenuity are helping to achieve new standards of performance, dependability, and economy.

### EATON
#### MANUFACTURING COMPANY
General Offices: CLEVELAND, OHIO

PLANTS: CLEVELAND  ·  MASSILLON
DETROIT  ·  SAGINAW  ·  BATTLE CREEK
MARSHALL  ·  LAWTON  ·  VASSAR
KENOSHA  ·  WINDSOR (CANADA)

*1950*

An Eaton ad from 1950 describes the company's many innovations over the years, including sodium-cooled valves, hydraulic valve lifters, rotor pumps, and Dynamatic drives.

---

innovations for passenger cars. Eaton's new offerings benefited from a growing middle class in the market for cars with luxury features.

In 1952, Eaton developed a rear window defroster available as both an add-on and a factory standard in several new car models. Installed in the shelf space behind a car's back seat, the defrosting unit was touted as a breakthrough because it defrosted and defogged "without causing drafts on the necks of passengers sitting in the rear seat," according to the *Eaton News*. A fan inside the defroster drew warm air from the car's interior and released it on the exterior of the rear window, warming the glass and causing ice and moisture to dissipate.[13]

A year later, Eaton engineers introduced a versatile ball bearing drive screw that debuted in Lincoln's new adjustable front seats. The heavy-duty, anti-friction screw could also be used in car windows, hoods, and convertible tops.[14] "By a mere touch of a button, the seat can be raised, lowered, or moved forward or backward at will," proclaimed an article in the *Eaton News*. "No more pulling or pushing or piling of cushions to get into the right driving positions. It is almost as if the hands of a dozen servants mysteriously wait on your needs."

Eaton researchers were also developing another innovation with multiple applications—the magnetic powder clutch. Propelled by a small amount of dry, lubricated magnetic powder, these drives were a significant improvement over older oil-powered magnetic clutches, which were rarely used in automobiles because the gears would heat up and quickly break down the oil suspension. Eaton engineers discovered that powdered iron would work better than liquid lubrication, and they added dry lubricants such as graphite and chalk to prevent the powder from clumping.

In 1954, *Popular Science* writer Frank Rowsome Jr. test drove a semiautomatic Ford Nash outfitted with Eaton's prototype magnetic powder clutch. "Right away, you notice the difference," he wrote. "When you put an ordinary automatic in drive, there is a subterranean *ka-chung* to tell you the plumbing is ready, a kind of false eagerness in the box."

Eaton's clutch, on the other hand, gave the driver full control of the transmission.[15] Rowsome called Eaton's clutch "lightning fast and sensitive," adding that, although simple, it had the potential to "revolutionize U.S. automatic transmissions."[16]

Magnetic powder clutches were used in other Eaton innovations as well. "We feel the product will be very important to our business in the future," noted Eaton's 1953 Annual Report. The magnetic clutch was also in production for highly classified applications with the U.S. military.[17]

As early as 1951, Eaton engineers from Central Research and the Heater Division began developing a car air conditioner that could shut off when it was not in use, an innovation made possible thanks to the magnetic clutch. Before the development of

# FULLER MANUFACTURING

FULLER MANUFACTURING Company was considered one of Eaton's most important, and most profitable, acquisitions. Fuller was founded as the Michigan Automobile Company in 1902 in Kalamazoo, Michigan. It originally specialized in manufacturing a lightweight, single-cylinder car with wire wheels called the Michigan. By 1908, however, the company had switched to manufacturing auto components, most notably transmissions and clutches.

In 1913, Michigan Automobile Company went through a significant reorganization and changed its name to Fuller and Sons Manufacturing. During this period, Fuller developed a heavy-duty truck transmission to serve the growing truck market. By 1923, the company had begun to focus exclusively on truck transmissions.[1] Throughout the 1930s, 1940s, and 1950s, many commercial trucks were equipped with Fuller transmissions and Eaton axles.[2]

In 1950, Fuller introduced the innovative 10-speed Roadranger transmission, which soon became wildly successful.[3] An 8-speed model introduced in 1953 also proved popular. Just a

Models R-96, R-960

**RoadRanger** TRANSMISSIONS

New ALUMINUM

the *LIGHTEST* 10-speed transmissions in trucking

New aluminum housings cut transmission weight by 160 pounds. In addition to this big weight reduction, these 10-speed ROADRANGERS offer:

- No gear splitting—10 selective ratios, evenly and progressively spaced.
- Easier, quicker shifts—28% steps between ratios.
- One shift lever controls all 10 forward and 2 reverse speeds.
- Engines operate in peak hp range with greater fuel economy.
- Range shifts pre-selected—automatic and synchronized.
- Less driver fatigue—½ less shifting.
- Compact space-and-weight-saving economies—the lightest, most compact 10-speed transmissions available.

See your truck dealer now . . . or write Fuller Manufacturing Company for complete details.

SAE JOURNAL, JULY, 1958

few years after being acquired by Eaton in 1958, Fuller introduced a Roadranger-branded twin countershaft transmission with a floating main shaft, the first of its kind. In 1966, Fuller expanded its manufacturing facilities to increase its output of Roadranger transmissions. In the ensuing years, Eaton took full advantage of the goodwill associated with Roadranger. In fact, by 2010, the Roadranger brand had been expanded to encompass a whole range of popular products, including brakes, driveshafts, and even energy-efficient hybrid systems. According to Thomas O'Boyle, retired group president of

Eaton's Truck Group, the Roadranger transmission revolutionized the industry. "They were able to get five, six times the life out of [a transmission] that weighed half as much, was much shorter, and gave the truck manufacturers just an absolute heyday in terms of being able to fit the product in," O'Boyle added. "They had so much room left over when they put that smaller product in, that they could do all kinds of other things underneath the chassis."[4]

According to future Eaton Chairman and CEO Bill Butler, Eaton purchased Fuller and its subsidiary Shuler Axle at an advantageous time. Just before Eaton acquired Fuller in 1958, President Dwight D. Eisenhower signed the National Interstate and Defense Highways Act of 1956, clearing the way for the construction of numerous interstate highways that proved a major boon to the truck industry. "We had, with this twin countershaft transmission, the perfect transmission for those long-distance runs," O'Boyle explained. "Eaton just blossomed after we got that product on the market and the superhighways were built."[5]

Eaton's new clutch, AC units would run continually at engine speeds, which drained the battery, wasted gas and horsepower, and caused unnecessary wear and tear on the compressor.

First tested in Florida in 1952, Eaton's air conditioner prototype was originally contained in a case mounted in the trunk. By 1955, Eaton had developed Eaton front-end AC units sold in Sears, Roebuck, & Company stores under the name Allstate. They were designed for use in vehicles manufactured by Ford, Mercury, Buick, Chevrolet, Oldsmobile, Cadillac, Pontiac, and Plymouth.[18]

Eaton's air-conditioning units were groundbreaking—the first car air conditioners affordable for the average consumer.[19] They proved incredibly popular, especially in the South and Southwest. By 1956, the Heater Division plant in Cleveland that manufactured the units was expanded to meet the increasing demand. Half of the new 60,000-square-foot addition to the plant was devoted to air-conditioning manufacturing.[20] According to the *Eaton News*, "Within a few years, 10 percent of all cars on the road will be equipped with air-conditioning."

Eaton also expanded its capabilities to include power steering and, propelled by the success of its magnetic powder clutch, spent $500,000 to

Cleveland Worm & Gear, the first U.S. company to mass-produce worm gearing, is pictured here in 1956. Eaton acquired the company and its subsidiary, Farval Corporation, in 1959.

acquire a plant in Coldwater, Michigan, for use in powdered metal research and production. The Coldwater plant applied powdered metal technology to the manufacture of automotive, aeronautical, and appliance parts, as well as carbide tools.[21]

With the opening of the Coldwater plant, Eaton became the only U.S. company that produced its own tungsten carbide—an extremely hard metal with a high melting point, used in the manufacture of machine tools.[22]

## Diversification

In the mid-1950s, Eaton grew by expanding its existing divisions and through several important acquisitions, becoming more efficient while diversifying its product offerings. Passenger car sales had begun to decline, further emphasizing Eaton's need to diversify. At the same time, some carmakers began to manufacture their components in-house, a practice Eaton tried to discourage. "Every time this happens, we make every effort to convince [automobile manufacturers] that through our facilities, know-how, and research, we can make a better product more economically," noted an article in the *Eaton News*.[23]

Although an increase in demand for heavy truck parts helped offset the decreased demand for passenger cars, Eaton recognized the continued need for diversification. As a result, according to the *Eaton News*, the company began making acquisitions "in fields we know best, adding new customers as well."[24]

In 1953, Eaton acquired the Spring Perch Company of Lackawanna, New York, a longtime supplier for Eaton's chassis springs. In addition to Eaton's Detroit plant, the acquisition of the Lackawanna facility in upstate New York allowed Eaton to more efficiently supply parts to its thriving Ontario operation, which had undergone a significant expansion in 1950.[25] In 1955, Eaton made two more significant acquisitions: Fredric Flader Inc. of North Tonawanda, New York, and Automotive Gear Works of Richmond, Indiana.

Fredric Flader Inc. focused almost exclusively on innovation. The company was named after founder Fredric Flader, a former Air Force engineer and a 1920 graduate of the Carnegie Institute of Technology. In 1944, Fredric Flader led a small team of engineers working on the Manhattan Project. Traveling between testing facilities at Cornell University in upstate New York and Los Alamos, New Mexico, Flader's research group helped design the structure of the atomic bomb, as well as the delivery aircraft's carrying and releasing gear.[26]

According to the *Eaton News*, under tight security, Flader had arranged for a secret room at Cornell's Curtiss-Wright Research Laboratory, "where one of the bombs, without fissionable material, was subject to numerous tests. The bomb was dropped some thousand times under every conceivable condition of plane altitude, vibration, heat, and cold."[27]

Flader then went on to work for the U.S. Air Force, designing and building the largest turbojet engine of its kind at that time before founding his own company.

When Eaton acquired the company, Fredric Flader Inc. had just completed an $875,000 upgrade of its machinery and had firmly established itself as a leader in developing and building experimental prototypes for turbojets, gas turbine engines, and nuclear power plants. Customers included Pratt & Whitney Aircraft, Curtiss-Wright, Westinghouse Electric, and Bell Aircraft. Thanks in part to the Fredric Flader Inc. acquisition, by 1957, Eaton

Pictured here is an assortment of chassis leaf springs, coil springs, and wire forms produced by Eaton's Spring Division in 1953.

# E. MANDELL DE WINDT

DURING HIS 17 YEARS AS chairman, E. Mandell "Del" de Windt transformed Eaton from a U.S. company primarily producing auto parts to an international corporation with subsidiaries in 21 countries and half of all sales coming from electrical, electronics, and defense products.

In 1978, he oversaw the acquisition of electrical company Cutler-Hammer, which would become one of Eaton's largest and most profitable product lines.[1] "I think of Del as the father of contemporary Eaton," said Stephen Hardis, Eaton's longtime chief financial officer and future chairman and CEO. "When he became CEO, he had an intuitive sense that being an automotive components supplier wasn't the way of the future. He made some important acquisitions, and tried to diversify through product development."[2]

In 1941, de Windt began working as a production clerk in Eaton's Battle Creek valve plant. He had completed just two years at Williams College, J. O. Eaton's alma mater, and was ready to try something new. When he heard J. O. Eaton was interested in hiring Williams graduates to work at Eaton, de Windt quit school and paid J. O. Eaton a visit. "I figured two more years of political science or economics wasn't going to do a hell of a lot for me," de Windt recalled. "It wasn't a large college, and I was bored. I had done about everything there I could do."[3]

J. O. Eaton offered him a choice of working either as a toolmaker's apprentice making $14 a week or a production clerk making $80 a month. "It didn't take me long to figure out which paid more," de Windt recalled. "I decided I had better be a production clerk."

His leadership skills soon became evident as he created the first Eaton personnel manual and developed a plan for rehiring soldiers returning from World War II. He was soon promoted to manager of the Stamping Division, and in 1959 he was named vice president of sales.

In 1961, de Windt's recommendation for consolidating Eaton's international operations propelled him to the position of president of Eaton International. In 1964, he became a director at the company, and three years later was elected Eaton president.[4] He retired from Eaton in 1986.

According to CEO and Chairman Sandy Cutler:

*Del envisioned a diversified Eaton. Under his leadership, Eaton bought the hydraulics business. Eaton bought Cutler-Hammer and Eaton Kenway. He was the catalyst for Eaton's global growth. Del was looking for a means to complement Eaton's strong automotive and truck businesses, and I think for many of his years as chairman, he was searching for the most promising industries.[5]*

had $221 million in annual sales, with major gains in passenger cars and aircraft components.

Flader was named general manager of the new Eaton division, which in 1957 began testing new automatic pneumatic brakes.[28] The 1957 Annual Report remarked on Fredric Flader Inc.'s "fine staff of research engineers devoting their efforts mainly to the aircraft industry," and predicted that Eaton would benefit from "new products that may be developed by the subsidiary."[29]

Meanwhile, Automotive Gear Works, based in Richmond, Indiana, specialized in manufacturing gears for farm and general industrial equipment. Automotive Gear founder Charles Edgar Hamilton had long been an active member of Eaton's board, serving for many years before the acquisition.[30]

Founded in 1941 in Atlanta, Georgia, Automotive Gear originally focused on manufacturing replacement parts. The company moved to Richmond in 1943 to be closer to the automobile industry, which accounted for 10 percent of the company's production.[31] The Richmond location, noted the *Eaton News*, allowed the engineering staff "to keep informed on every trend of machine tool design."[32]

"This manufacturer of a broad line of gears fit our pattern of expansion, with a major diversification benefit—more than 60 percent of the plant's output goes into fields other than automotive," explained E. L. Ludvigsen, Eaton board member and future chairman.

According to Ludvigsen, Eaton searched for acquisition opportunities that "would carry our particular capabilities into new markets," while avoiding acquisitions that would "violate our relationships with the automotive industry, where our traditions were established and our future bright."[33]

As the *Eaton News* explained, with 300 employees, Automotive Gear Works proved an ideal size, "large enough to give excellent service and mass-production economies, and yet small enough to give, when necessary, highly individualized technical assistance."[34]

R. H. Daisley, vice president–administrative and longtime member of the board, told the Richmond Rotary Club that a major part of Automotive Gear Works' appeal was that it remained a growing company, "one which is part of an industry that has a definite future, well established in its particular field and able to withstand any temporary setback, and whose management is alert."[35]

In 1958, Eaton made another major acquisition, this time in the truck components field. The acquisition of Fuller Manufacturing Company, the 56-year-old firm based in Kalamazoo, Michigan, allowed Eaton to offer customers a full line of medium- and heavy-duty transmissions along with Eaton's popular axles. According to Eaton's 1958 Annual Report, the acquisition "entrenched [Eaton's] position in the truck components field" and improved compatibility between transmissions and driving rear axles.[36]

Complementing the Fuller acquisition was the acquisition of its subsidiary the Shuler Axle Company, a leading supplier of front steering axles, commercial trailer axles, and air brakes. Founded in 1915 in Louisville, Kentucky, Shuler pioneered heavy-duty aluminum brakes and lightweight magnesium brakes and hubs. After the acquisition, Eaton invested $650,000 into expanding the Shuler plant.[37]

Throughout the decade, Eaton continued to enter new markets. The company hired an independent market research firm that produced a study describing pleasure boating as a growth industry. Eaton took the prediction to heart and began manufacturing products for these types of boats, including its Interceptor Marine Engines and the Eaton Powernaut Drive. The company also acquired Dearborn Marine Engines Inc.

John Virden served as Eaton chairman from 1957 to 1967. A former director of the Federal Reserve Bank of Cleveland, he was appointed to Eaton's board in 1948 and promptly visited every Eaton plant at his own expense to learn more about the company.

of Michigan, which manufactured inboard engines for pleasure boats.

Eaton's diversification efforts soon began to pay off, and sales steadily increased on automotive air-conditioning systems, components, and magnetic clutches. The Heater Division developed plastic parts for heaters and air conditioners. Eaton also introduced the Dyna-torQ, a new line of magnetically actuated, friction-type clutches and brakes. By the late 1950s, Eaton was organized into 10 divisions: Heater, Dynamatic, Axle, Saginaw, Stamping, Automotive Gear, Spring, Pump, Aircraft, and Research.

### Working Union Issues

Despite posting record production rates and revenue in the early part of the decade, the automobile industry experienced a slump toward the end of the 1950s. The high cost of steel, rising

---

Eaton acquired Fuller Manufacturing subsidiary Shuler Axle in 1958. Pictured here is the Shuler assembly plant. *(Photo by Manning Studios, Inc.)*

labor costs, a backlog in inventory after a production surge in 1953, and a gradual shift in consumer tastes from luxury cars to smaller, more economical models all contributed to a slowdown in industry profits. Changes emerged in the auto industry that would reverberate for the next half-century.

According to the *New York Times*:

*Lagging auto sales, particularly in the medium-priced lines, are prompting reappraisals of the public's attitudes toward automobiles. Do people want expensive, chrome-covered, prestige-laden big cars, or do they want more economical basic transportation? ... The growing popularity of the small economy car may force the Big Three automakers to enter this field, which they have previously scorned. Both Ford and General Motors are reported to be planning small cars that may reach the production stage by 1960 provided the market for such cars holds up.*[38]

New car inventories soared to record heights, saddling car dealerships with more models than they could sell.[39] In response, by early 1954, automobile manufacturers began instituting plant

# INTERNATIONAL GROWTH

EATON'S GLOBAL EXPANSION AND diversification efforts during the late 1950s and early 1960s ultimately led to the company's decision to create a separate business segment devoted to international growth. The company had a long history of entering foreign markets, with operating plants in Canada since the 1930s and ventures in the United Kingdom in the 1940s.

In 1957, Eaton teamed up with a Brazilian engineering and construction firm to form Eaton S.A. Corp. in Brazil, which supplied automotive engine valves to Ford. A year later, Eaton launched a second South American subsidiary called Fuller do Brasil and built a factory for the production of truck transmissions.[1] Eaton continued its expansion efforts in South America in 1961, opening a new truck axle plant near Buenos Aires, Argentina, under a new subsidiary called Eaton Ejes, I.C.S.A.

Eaton next turned to Italy in 1961, acquiring a majority interest in Livia, S.p.A., in Turin, the country's largest independent maker of automotive engine valves.[2] Eaton actually had a presence in Italy since 1953, when it entered into a licensing agreement with Livia for producing engine valves. Within a few years, Livia supplied all of French automaker Simca's engine and valve components for all Fiat truck engines. When Eaton acquired its majority

interest in Livia in 1961, it officially entered the European Common Market as a manufacturer.

To better manage its foreign enterprises, in 1961 Eaton formed an umbrella operation known as Eaton International. Future Eaton chairman Del de Windt, then vice president of sales, suggested the move. Under de Windt's direction, Eaton set up operations in more than 20 other countries.

While Eaton originally brought over managers from the United States to run plants overseas, the company found that production increased when it placed local managers in charge. Eaton soon instituted a successful, long-running policy of combining the best local talent with the ideas and experience of Eaton's engineering and marketing personnel in the United States.[3]

shutdowns for several days each week. At the same time, the auto industry responded to declining market conditions and began increasing factory automation. Unions reacted negatively to these changes. The United Auto Workers (UAW) union began pushing automakers to adopt a guaranteed annual wage provision, which would have forced manufacturers to compensate workers for the difference between their regular wages and any unemployment losses if they were laid off during temporary plant shutdowns. Although the guaranteed annual wage provision was never fully adopted, the battle between the unions and automakers quickly turned bitter,

contributing to work stoppages throughout the auto industry.[40]

The labor unrest soon affected Eaton, which employed many UAW workers. In 1955, after Ford and GM made concessions to laid-off workers, Eaton agreed to a supplemental layoff package for its 4,100 UAW workers that included wage increases, better insurance, medical benefits, and more overtime pay.[41] Despite Eaton's efforts, in August 1955, workers went on a nine-week strike at Eaton's Axle Division plant in Cleveland. Eaton's Annual Report that year said only that the strike "did not develop from the economic package

Eaton had many company bowling leagues in the 1950s. Pictured here is the Axle Division women's league in Cleveland circa 1951.

offered by the company, but from the union's resistance to changes in working conditions which were necessary to maintain the right of management to control the plant. [It] was a costly experience for all involved."[42]

Eaton Axle Division employees went on strike again for four weeks in 1957, and yet again in 1958, a year in which the company experienced "numerous work stoppages," according to the 1958 Annual Report. With union contracts up for renewal, new three-year agreements were ultimately negotiated successfully, "but some of the settlements came only after strike shutdowns in five [Eaton] plants represented by the United Auto Workers, and one plant represented by the International Association of Machinists."[43]

Meanwhile, costs continued to rise, including significant increases in wages and benefits, higher prices for raw materials, and increasing freight rates. Despite Eaton's continued attempts to improve its manufacturing efficiency, the company was forced to pass on part of its higher costs to customers. However, profits continued to decline even as sales increased.[44]

Due to a desire to improve productivity and meet customer expectations, Eaton decided to open new plants in locations that offered much greater workforce flexibility. However, Eaton continued to suffer additional challenges. In 1959, a 116-day steelworkers' strike slowed down operations at many Eaton plants. The company had previously accumulated extra steel, in addition to the industry-standard 45-day inventory. However, Eaton still began to run short three months into the strike, forcing Eaton to cut back on production and to shut down plants.

Eaton would go on to build approximately 30 nonunion plants in southern and western states. According to future Eaton Chairman and CEO Bill Butler, "We tried to be as generous as we could with the existing employees in the plants while focusing on improving quality and maintaining flexibility."[45]

## A Global Company

By the end of the 1950s, Eaton had become a more efficient, diversified company. Since World War II, Eaton had spent more than $100 million on expansion. Eaton's product lines were sold to more than 50 different industries, including truck, passenger car, machine tool, and industrial machinery manufacturing, as well as manufacturers of electrical equipment, farm machinery, aircraft, material handling, railroad, and construction and road-building equipment.

Eaton had already been operating plants in Canada since the 1930s and had also previously invested in Europe. In 1946, Eaton had acquired a minority interest in Hobourn-Eaton Manufacturing Company Ltd., a British manufacturer of motor pumps and gears, and in 1947, Eaton and two British companies, axle maker Rubery Owen & Company Ltd. and truck axle and gear maker ENV Engineering Company Ltd., had formed a sales and engineering joint venture that supplied parts to Ford and General Motors in England.

The late 1950s, however, marked Eaton's first entry into South America. In 1957, the company launched Eaton S.A. Corp. in Brazil—a joint venture with a Brazilian engineering and construction firm. Initially, the 25,000-square-foot plant in São Paulo manufactured automotive engine valves. According to the 1957 Annual Report, the company hoped to expand its Brazilian operations "to make other Eaton parts for present and new customers who have passenger car and truck plants in Brazil or are planning to construct such facilities. ... We regard Brazil as a growth country, industrially and economically."[46]

Just one year later, Eaton began an ambitious expansion of its Brazilian operations, forming a second subsidiary called Fuller do Brasil and building a new plant for manufacturing truck transmissions.[47] In 1959, Eaton finished paying off the last of its remaining debt from its purchase of Fuller and the board of directors announced a two-for-one stock split to its 17,389 shareholders. By 1960, Eaton had 23 manufacturing divisions and subsidiaries, 33 plants, and two research and development centers devoted to new products and production equipment for its factories. Eaton had begun the transformation from a specialized U.S. automotive parts company to a diversified international corporation.

In 1964, Eaton moved to its new Cleveland headquarters at the Erieview Tower office building, affectionately dubbed the "Jolly Green Giant."

## CHAPTER SIX

# GOING GLOBAL
## 1961 – 1967

*Because our engineered products have a long life and require a lengthy lead time from design concept to marketplace, planning for tomorrow demands a high degree of technological sophistication.*

—Eaton 1967 Annual Report[1]

THROUGHOUT THE 1960s, EATON continued to strengthen its presence abroad. A strong dollar made foreign acquisitions especially attractive. In addition, major new highway construction projects in Argentina, Mexico, Brazil, Spain, West Germany, and Great Britain created new demand for components involved in the production of passenger cars, trucks, and heavy machinery.[2] By 1961, Eaton's international prospects flourished as the company launched a separate international division to manage its growing overseas operations, which by then included 600 employees and 155,000 square feet of manufacturing space.[3] E. Mandell "Del" de Windt, Eaton's vice president of sales at the time, was promoted to president of the company's new Eaton International Division after proposing the consolidation.[4]

A number of Eaton's U.S. customers, including Ford, Chrysler, General Motors, and International Harvester, encouraged Eaton to establish overseas manufacturing facilities to support their international operations. In a 1962 letter to U.S. employees, de Windt addressed Eaton's need to further increase its global reach:

*Many of us can remember the day when U.S. companies could competitively export their goods to practically every foreign country, [but] the free countries of the world are now on the move. Each has its own plan to develop its industry, to create jobs for its people, and to raise living standards. If we want their business, we must be on the scene. Otherwise, we may find ourselves locked out of their markets in the future.[5]*

Eaton International's relationships with vehicle manufacturers abroad in turn benefited its U.S. operations. Volvo, for instance, had a license to manufacture Eaton axles for its trucks in Europe. However, according to de Windt, when supplies ran low, Volvo purchased additional parts from Eaton plants in the United States, "to such an extent that Volvo has ranked for many years as one of our key customers."[6]

Eaton's Foundry Division developed new methods to manufacture high alloy castings for sophisticated equipment such as turbine engines.

During the 1960s, Eaton's Shuler Axle subsidiary completed a $500,000 expansion that increased production capacity by 30 percent.

Eaton first entered the European Common Market as a manufacturer in May 1961 by acquiring a majority interest in Eaton Livia S.p.A., Italy's largest independent engine valve maker. That same year, Eaton made further inroads into Great Britain when it acquired a minority interest in Eaton Axles Ltd., a truck axle manufacturer and Eaton licensee since the 1940s.[7]

In 1962, after England announced its national highway construction project, Eaton borrowed $20 million to acquire British company ENV Engineering.[8] At the time, ENV was one of the largest manufacturers of transmissions, axle components, and gears for trucks, automobiles, and aircraft in Great Britain. It also exported much of its production to Scandinavia. Like Eaton, ENV had a long history in the vehicle components industry and was founded in 1910, just a year before J. O. Eaton began selling Torbensen Axle components.[9]

In 1962, subsidiary Eaton Ejes I.C.S.A. of Argentina began constructing a plant near Buenos Aires that specialized in axles for the Argentine subsidiaries of U.S. vehicle manufacturers.[10] The expansion proved particularly prescient. By 1964, Argentine law required that 70

percent of the components in all trucks and 90 percent of components for all passenger cars sold in Argentina be manufactured within the country. Eaton benefited since it already had a significant strategic foothold in the market.

Brazil also changed its laws, with new regulations requiring that 98 percent of all new trucks be manufactured within the country. Since Eaton had established operations in Brazil during the late 1950s as part of a joint venture with Brazilian investors, the company remained well positioned to take advantage of the new opportunities.[11] With successful operations in Europe, Great Britain, and Latin America, Eaton executives set their sights on Asia and the Pacific Rim. In response, de Windt proposed entering India and the Australian market, where Eaton had previously licensed its products.[12]

## Expanding Through Acquisitions

By 1961, trucks hauled 22 percent of America's freight, a fourfold increase compared to 1945 figures. Eaton was up to the challenge of meeting the burgeoning demand and developed the world's first successful three-speed tandem axle. When used with a five-speed transmission, the three-speed axle gave truck operators the choice of 15 forward speeds. "For each transmission gear, a driver has three very close gear steps—low, intermediate, and high—which give him a broader selection of the best gear ratios for the terrain and load he is carrying," explained an article in the *Eaton News*. "In effect, the three-speed tandem axle gives a driver 50 percent more selectivity of gear ratios."[13]

The axle featured a fingertip lever that could be operated with the thumb or index finger, making it easy to shift. The Fuller Division also manufactured an optional companion five-speed transmission for the axle.

At the time, Eaton faced increasing competition from other firms even as some carmakers began manufacturing their own components. Eaton maintained its competitive edge by relying on innovations such as the three-speed axle, industrial power transmissions, and advanced air-conditioning systems.[14] Eaton also carefully chose acquisitions to build its strength in strategic areas, often acquiring companies that had been in business for decades, and focusing on manufacturers specializing in building components that complemented Eaton's existing product lines.[15]

In 1961, Eaton acquired Dill Manufacturing of Cleveland, a 52-year-old company and one of the country's most successful producers of tire valves, valve parts, accessories, and related equipment for cars, trucks, and heavy equipment.[16] Founders Arthur Williamson, Peter R. Dill, and Paul H. Brandt created the company in 1909 with a loan from Williamson's father. By 1924, the company had grown into a large operation, manufacturing 4 million valve stems and 5.5 million valve components annually. The company had continued to thrive even during the Great Depression by shifting its focus to selling replacement tires and Dillectric patching tubes."[17]

By 1961, Dill had 500 employees and 155,000 square feet of plant space in the United States and Canada.[18] It was the largest U.S. manufacturer of valve cores, which were used in many different applications, including vehicle suspension systems, automatic watering troughs, and release-mechanisms for oxygen masks in Boeing jets. "Dill produces many different types of tube and tubeless tire valves, tire pressure gauges, repair, and related equipment, but the heart of the business is still the tiny, simple valve," noted the Eaton News at the time of the acquisition.[19]

In early 1963, Eaton acquired another complementary manufacturer, the 57-year-old Dole Valve Company. Based in the Chicago suburb of Morton Grove, Illinois, it was a leading manufacturer of appliance and automotive controls, plumbing and heating valves, and beverage dispensers. Dole got its start in 1906, selling packless radiator valves for steam heating systems. In 1921, it built its first factory on Chicago's West Side. The company gradually expanded by manufacturing gasoline and oil line fittings for automobiles and soon won an important contract to supply parts for Buick. Dole was also known for introducing the world's first automobile thermostat in 1924. The innovative technology would later be used in washing machines and drink dispensers.[20]

By 1963, Dole operated four plants in Illinois and had earned a reputation for making high quality thermostats, fuel line couplings, and starters.[21] With a strong presence in the industry, Dole proved

a perfect strategic acquisition that also helped Eaton diversify its offerings.[22]

## A New Day for Research

Eaton ramped up its research and development in 1961, dedicating a nine-acre research center in the Detroit suburb of Southfield, Michigan, to developing innovative new products. The $2.3 million state-of-the-art facility was dedicated to creating new products and improving existing ones. Described in the Eaton News as "the physical expression of Eaton's conviction that research is the foundation of industrial progress," the center was equipped with a machine shop, a radioisotope laboratory, a brake-testing facility, an instrumentation room, a stress study room, and a road-test garage. In addition, the facility featured an ingenious fatigue-testing machine capable of "simulating a fully loaded truck

Eaton acquired the Trojan brand of heavy-duty construction equipment as part of the Yale & Towne acquisition in 1963. The company immediately began making significant investments, including purchasing new equipment such as the automatic flame cutter pictured here.

under the worst road conditions." The machine could destroy a large truck housing in just a few hours without causing any strain on the building.[23]

Products and manufacturing processes developed during this time included the controlled plating of hydraulic lifters to help prevent corrosion in car engines, more efficient engine cooling viscous fan drives, a line of humidifiers, and a compensating pulley for engine V-belts that automatically maintained the proper tension.[24]

With the Southfield research center up and running, Eaton's Central Research laboratory in South Euclid, Ohio, shifted its focus to the development of money-saving production techniques and was renamed the Eaton Technical Center.[25] Eaton had expanded its research and development efforts beyond automotive parts and accessories to include machine tool compo-

nents, lift trucks, marine engines and drives, and appliance controls. Other products in development during the mid-1960s included antilock brake controls designed to improve the stopping ability of large vehicles in bad weather and a riderless lift truck for automated warehouses.[26]

One of Eaton's key breakthroughs in the 1960s was the development of a cost-efficient hydrostatic transmission designed to decrease the amount of manual labor needed to operate farm vehicles. Unlike automatic transmissions, hydrostatic transmissions are operated by hydraulics instead of conventional gears. A series of pumps capable of varying fluid flow regulate power into the motor, resulting in a smoother ride and better acceleration—especially in heavy trucks and off-road vehicles such as tractors and construction equipment.

By 1967, Eaton was producing three Marshallmatic hydrostatic transmission models for the tractor market. The company predicted that within five years it would be producing 500,000 hydrostatic transmissions annually. To accommodate that growth, it expanded its Marshall Division with a 500,000-square-foot addition, along with opening a new proving ground for testing tractors and transmissions on a 400-acre farm nearby. Plans called for the company to develop the transmissions for

In 1961, Eaton opened a new research center in Southfield, Michigan.

Insets: The state-of-the-art Southfield, Michigan, research center included an instrumentation room (left) and a radioisotope laboratory (right).

vehicles ranging from 4 to 200 horsepower.[27]

In 1967, Eaton researchers partnered with Ford Motor Company engineers to develop one of the first passenger car air bag systems. Known as the Auto-Ceptor restraint system, it featured "balloonlike bags triggered to inflate automatically upon collision," noted an article in the trade magazine *Steel*. Upon impact, a sensor released gas to inflate the bags. Perforations in the bags' sides then "caused instant deflation to gently ease the riders forward."[28]

Eaton estimated the passive restraint system could save more than 25,000 lives each year, twice as many as seat belts alone. However, the technology garnered mixed reactions. The U.S. Department of Transportation was confident enough in the technology that it installed air bags in 5,000 of its vehicles.[29] "The front seat air bag, hailed by some advocates as the greatest automotive safety device ever developed, is the chief reason for the current popularity of [Eaton] among investors," stated an article in the *New York Times*.[30]

However, the added costs of the air bag system led to resistance from manufacturers and the public.[31] Eaton ultimately sold the rights for the air bag restraint system to TRW. Although the bags were first introduced in American cars in the 1970s, they did not become standard automobile safety devices until the 1990s, and have since been adopted for widespread use.

In 1967, Eaton developed and tested the Auto-Ceptor, one of the world's first air bag systems.

### Gearing Up for the Computer Age

Eaton had installed its first computer, an IBM 650, as early as 1955, when there were fewer than 1,000 working computers in the United States. It was originally used for payroll, inventory, and production control, mainly at the Eaton Axle Division. The company soon began integrating data processing equipment into its regular operations. Two years later, Eaton's computer systems had become sophisticated enough to warrant a move to a full-fledged computer center in a two-story building on Cleveland's northeast side. It housed the Burroughs 205 system, a massive early computer that used vacuum tubes that could complete a two-hour pen-and-paper calculation job in a matter of minutes.[32]

Globally, Eaton began developing a communications network connecting satellite computers at its Italian, German, Canadian, British, and American plants in 1967. The hub was a telecomputer center in the Cleveland suburb of Eastlake. Employing 150 people, the center was intended to showcase the latest in computer technology for international visitors, according to the *Eaton News*. Innovations included computer graphics, numerical controls, and automatic message switching.[33]

### Yale & Towne

In 1963, Eaton purchased the renowned 95-year-old firm Yale & Towne Manufacturing Co., its largest acquisition up to that point. Yale

# THE EATON PHILOSOPHY

IN 1968, EATON EMBARKED ON a new approach to running a factory that would revolutionize the company's corporate culture.[1] At the time, there was a "we and them" attitude common throughout the industry. However, that mentality was not productive and Eaton began to search for a better way to do business.[2]

The result of those efforts was the Eaton Philosophy, a set of standards intended to bring out the best in every employee, creating a fulfilling and enriching workplace atmosphere that encourages and rewards contributions made by staff at every level of the company.

The initial impetus for the Eaton Philosophy began with the founding of a new engine valve plant in Kearney, Nebraska. "In developing plans for the new plant, Eaton set out to avoid the adversarial relations between management and the workforce that characterized the American auto industry at that time," explained Vice President of Human Resource Programs Steve Bartlett in 2010. "Out of that determination was born something initially called the 'new philosophy.'"[3]

Eaton chose to pursue what was considered a groundbreaking idea at the time. Starting with the Kearney plant, the Eaton Philosophy was extended to all manufacturing facilities. The new philosophy broke down the usual divisions between management and employees as it was applied and adapted to all global facilities. In a sense, all of Eaton's employees would now be treated as equals, regardless of position, and everyone would be given the opportunity to make their voices heard on all major decisions regarding employee policies. According to one Eaton manager at the time, "I can no longer conceive of making a decision of major impact without first inviting meaningful dialogue."[4]

Eaton's new philosophy had immediate benefits, including a remarkable reduction in absenteeism and employee turnover alongside a jump in productivity reaching as high as 35 percent. The company soon began implementing the approach in all of its new facilities, with 13 new plants following the new philosophy by 1975.[5]

The Eaton Philosophy significantly improved the relationship between managers and employees, focusing on building a foundation of teamwork and trust based on the assumption that everybody at Eaton simply wanted to do their best.[6]

By 1985, Eaton officially introduced the Eaton Philosophy as a set of value statements and implemented it company-wide. As Eaton has grown to become a global powerhouse, these value statements have been revised to help guide the company and its employees. They have been translated into 32 languages.

## The Eaton Philosophy: Excellence Through People

The Eaton Philosophy is built on the fundamental belief that all employees genuinely want to contribute their best and do what's right. Our policies, practices, and decisions reflect this fundamental principle.

### Excellence:
### We strive to be the best.

*We expect the best of people and take personal responsibility for the quality of everything we do. We set high standards of excellence for the products we make, the service* we provide, and our working relationships. To achieve our goals, we remove barriers to speed and efficiency without compromising quality.

### Accountability:
### We keep our commitments.

We honor our commitments to achieve superior results for our customers, shareholders, and one another. By setting clear and measurable objectives that are aligned with the business, we are fully accountable for individual and organizational performance. In so doing, we embrace continuous feedback and coaching to improve our performance and to help us realize our full potential.

### Health and Safety:
### We are committed to the well being of all employees.

We are committed to sustaining a safe workplace. Our practices, processes, and decisions reflect our inherent belief in the well being of our employees, their families, and communities. We are responsible not only for our own safety, but the safety of others. This commitment is also reflected in our portfolio of quality products and services.

### Inclusion:
### We value individual differences.

Our success depends on our ability to draw the very best people from the global, cross-cultural talent pool reflecting the diversity of our customers, communities, and markets. We foster an inclusive environment that respects individual differences and values the unique perspectives that lead to innovative ideas and better decisions.

### Communication:
### We communicate openly and honestly.

We provide timely and candid communications to share information, make good decisions, and do our jobs effectively. Formal and informal communication channels are used to raise new ideas, share feedback that improves the business, and voice concerns about workplace issues that affect us.

### Compensation:
### We provide competitive pay and benefits.

We provide competitive total compensation that includes pay and benefits consistent with the varied compensation practices in different regions of the world. An array of programs and tools are utilized to recognize individual and group achievements and to enable us to reward performance consistent with our contributions.

### Learning:
### We continuously learn, grow, and change.

Accelerating change in our global markets requires us to embrace new ideas and continuously adapt to new challenges to meet rising customer expectations. We utilize the resources and support available to learn, apply new skills, and pursue opportunities for self-development.

### Innovation:
### We value new ideas.

Our success depends on driving continuous improvement and creating innovative new products and services that differentiate us from our competition. We encourage ideas that add value to the way we work as well as the solutions we provide our customers. An environment where new and innovative ideas can flourish is vital to our ultimate success.

### Engagement:
### We are involved in our work and committed to Eaton's future.

High performance and job satisfaction result when employees are fully engaged in their work and the business. We promote the participation and teamwork necessary for individuals to contribute fully to the organization.

### Environment and Communities:
### We strive to improve the environment and our communities.

We encourage involvement in our communities to build a positive environment for the workplace, our families, and the world around us. We support efforts to improve the environment and are committed to doing our share in creating and sustaining a "green world."

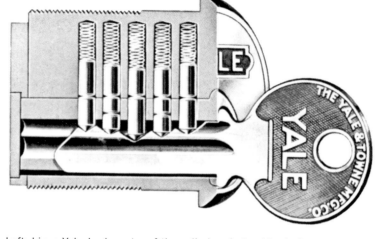

Left: Linus Yale Jr., inventor of the cylinder pin-tumbler lock (above), cofounded Yale & Towne in 1868.

Below: In 1919, Yale & Towne opened its first international plant in Canada. This illustration is from a 50th anniversary souvenir booklet.

& Towne manufactured lift trucks, electric hoists, and other materials handling equipment. The company was founded in 1868 by Linus Yale Jr., inventor of the now ubiquitous cylinder pin-tumbler lock.[34]

Yale & Towne opened its first Canadian plant in 1911 and its first European plant in Germany in 1922. In 1929, it acquired England's largest lock manufacturer, and in 1957, ventured into the construction equipment field, manufacturing rubber-tired front-end loaders.[35] At the time of the Eaton acquisition, Yale had 4,000 employees and a strong presence in the international market, with subsidiaries in England, West Germany, and Italy, as well as numerous partnerships and licensees worldwide.

According to Eaton Chairman E. L. Ludvigsen, "Yale & Towne's strong position in the materials handling equipment, locks, and hardware markets represented a significant extension of Eaton's broad diversification program as well as excellent potential for profitable growth."[36]

Soon after the acquisition, Eaton began making substantial investments in Yale & Towne, including the consolidation of Yale & Towne's New York headquarters in the Chrysler Building with Eaton's general offices. Eaton opened new, combined world headquarters in downtown

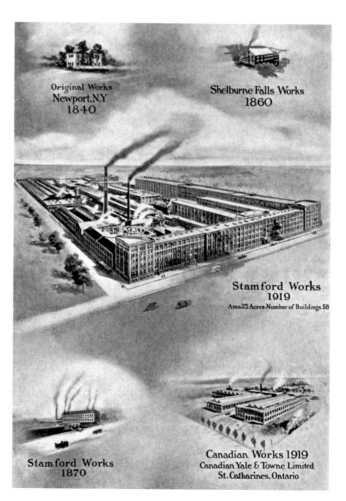

Cleveland at the 40-story Erieview Tower building, affectionately nicknamed the "Jolly Green Giant" due to its dark-green exterior.

Designed by the New York architectural firm of Harrison & Abramovitz (also the designers of Rockefeller Center and Lincoln Center), Erieview Tower was part of one of the era's most ambitious projects under a federal urban renewal program. For this undertaking, the City of Cleveland acquired a large block of land from E. 6th to E. 17th streets and Chester Avenue to Lake Erie and sold it to private developers. Developers then followed an urban master plan designed by famed architect I. M. Pei, who later designed Cleveland's Rock and Roll Hall of Fame and Museum and a new wing to the Louvre Museum in Paris.[37]

According to Eaton's 1964 Annual Report, the establishment of its new global headquarters was intended to streamline operations and cut down on administrative expenses.[38] Eaton also earmarked additional money for research and development. New areas of research included machine tool components, lift trucks, locks and hardware, marine engines and drives, and appliance controls. "With the rapid growth of Eaton's business in recent years, we are devoting larger budgets to our vital research and development program," stated the 1964 Annual Report.

In 1965, having grown to 35,000 employees, Eaton officially changed its name to Eaton Yale & Towne to reflect the melding of the two companies. "We wanted to retain one of the oldest and most respected names in the field of materials handling equipment and locks," explained Eaton's 1965 letter to shareholders.[39]

Unfortunately, the Yale & Towne acquisition ultimately proved unsuccessful. By 1971, Eaton had dropped the Yale & Towne name, officially becoming Eaton Corporation. A decade later, Eaton would divest itself of the last remaining Yale & Towne product lines.

Eaton also made several significant smaller acquisitions during the time period, including logging equipment manufacturer Timberjack Machines Ltd. of Woodstock, Ontario; Automated Handling Systems of Washington, D.C., designer of labor-saving systems for factories and nuclear waste transport systems; and the Fawick Corporation, maker of

In 1965, Eaton changed its name to Eaton Yale & Towne.

truck air brakes, hydroelectric control valves, and rubber golf club grips.[40]

## Eaton's International Efforts

By the mid-1960s, political turmoil in Brazil and Argentina led to losses in South America. However, Eaton's international business continued to flourish overall. In 1964, the company spent $5.8 million on plants and equipment to meet overseas demand for axles, transmissions, engine valves, and lift trucks. Eaton also entered Spain and Australia for the first time as a manufacturer, acquiring Eaton Valves (Australia) Pty. Ltd. in Sydney, and an equity interest in Eaton Ibérica S.A. of Pamplona, Spain.

Plants were also expanded and modernized in England, Italy, and Argentina to meet increased demand. New regional directors were named for British, European, and Latin American operations.[41] As Eaton expanded, it hired the majority of its overseas workers locally. According to the 1964 letter to shareholders, "In keeping with the practice of relying on nationals, the company today has fewer than 10 U.S. citizens in its foreign plants. The Brazilian and Argentine plants are managed and operated solely by local nationals."[42]

By 1965, Eaton had 31 international divisions, subsidiaries, and associated companies in Britain, West Germany, Italy, Spain, Argentina, Brazil, Colombia, Mexico, and Australia. The

# GLOBAL BUSINESS UNITS

DURING ITS EARLY ENTRY INTO the international sector, Eaton focused on supplying U.S. automakers with components for their overseas manufacturing operations. Although Eaton used local labor and materials, the components Eaton manufactured in its overseas facilities were identical to those built in the United States.

However, as Eaton grew and diversified into new markets, the company's international operations became more independent, allowing its overseas divisions to better respond to local market conditions, economic realities, and specific business cultures.[1] In 1968, Eaton integrated its international segments, research and development efforts, and marketing operations into five basic product groups: Truck and Off-Highway Components, Materials Handling, Automotive and Controls, Industrial Power Transmissions Systems and General Products, and Lock and Hardware.

According to Eaton's 1968 Annual Report, "This coordination of global efforts provides the company with a considerably strengthened base to increase worldwide penetration of the markets we serve, [moving Eaton closer] to true international status."[2]

Truck and Off-Highway Components was the largest group, accounting for 30 percent of annual sales. It focused on producing powertrain components for heavy-duty vehicles. Products included multispeed drive axles, transmissions, trailer axles, and braking and suspension systems.

Materials Handling consisted of the most diverse line of industrial lift trucks in the industry at the time. Eaton products included forklifts capable of handling up to 100 tons, lift trucks built to navigate tight turns in warehouses, logging vehicles, and tractors.

Eaton's passenger car components were grouped into the Automotive and Controls Group. These included engine components, safety accessories, tire valves, thermostats, and hydraulics.

Industrial Power Transmissions Systems and General Products consisted of factory automation products, along with miscellaneous products such as golf grips and multiuse fasteners. The Lock and Hardware Group, a product of the Yale & Towne acquisition, represented the smallest group, with 7 percent of annual sales. It included locks and hardware for builders, architects, manufacturers, retailers, and consumers.[3]

In the 40 years that followed, Eaton has continued to organize the company into four international business units, although the categories have been adjusted as unprofitable product lines were sold off, new products were developed, and new acquisitions were made. In 2010, Eaton's Global Business Units included Aerospace, Electrical, Hydraulics, and Vehicle.

Above: By the 1960s, the Eaton family had grown to encompass many well-known brands.

Right: In 1967, Eaton created a promotional brochure for the German market that highlighted the company's international manufacturing capabilities.

company also had 47 foreign licensees in 13 countries, manufacturing more than 50 Eaton products. All told, Eaton products were sold in 80 countries and international sales accounted for 17 percent of Eaton's total revenues.[43]

In 1966, the company launched its first truck axle plant in Mexico and sent its first shipment of axles to the Mexican subsidiaries of many U.S. automakers. Eaton's Mexico plants produced rear truck axles and steering assemblies for Ford, General Motors, and Chrysler. Eaton already benefited from its substantial minority ownership in three other companies there: Eaton Yale de Mexico S.A., Manufacturas Lock S.A., and Partes de Motor S.A.

With foreign sales growing as a percentage of revenue every year, Eaton began allowing its international side of the business to gain further autonomy. As de Windt explained:

*Very soon, these fledgling international plants acquired a life of their own. Under the impact of the different needs of a variety of markets, and of the economic facts of life in each of these, the products and the manufacturing methods had to change.*

*That meant our overseas operations had to develop their own engineering, manufacturing, and marketing capabilities, drawing on domestic know-how. This made them better able to deal with their immediate and local problems than the people in our domestic divisions could.*[44]

By the late 1960s, the specialized components Eaton manufactured in foreign markets differed substantially from its U.S. products. The 47 international operations in 18 countries were "expanding rapidly under their own steam," de Windt explained. "Now there is a constant exchange of ideas between our domestic and international plants."

Although conditions in the automobile market proved less favorable toward the end of the decade, Eaton had grown and diversified so much that by 1969 the company hit the $1 billion sales mark. Eaton remained firmly on the path toward success as a groundbreaking global corporation.[45]

# Change
# through innovation...
## the world over

**FAT•N**

Eaton's 1973 promotional book, *Change Through Innovation*, highlighted the company's increasing global reach.

## CHAPTER SEVEN

# OVERCOMING CHALLENGES
## 1968 – 1979

*Effective strategic planning demands that we constantly evaluate our current businesses and their performance against planned objectives.*

—1977 Letter to Shareholders[1]

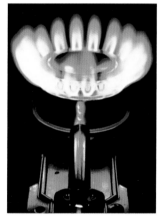

BY THE LATE 1960s, EATON'S INTERNAtional business had grown so large and complex that its product lines were integrated into five basic groups in an effort to better coordinate operations. The divisions included Truck and Off-Highway Components, Materials Handling, Automotive and Controls, Industrial Power Transmissions Systems and General Products, and Lock and Hardware. The new level of organization allowed Eaton's overseas operations to maintain a large degree of autonomy in daily decisions, while still preserving an organizational structure that remained consistent worldwide.[2]

It proved an important decision, made at a crucial time. With domestic profits slowing, Eaton began devoting more resources to expanding its overseas operations. In 1968, the company ventured into Japan, signing a licensing agreement with Sumitomo Machinery Co. Ltd. a major manufacturing operation based in Osaka. The agreement granted Sumitomo Japanese manufacturing rights for Eaton's Trojan brand of materials handling and construction equipment.[3]

Eaton also made new inroads into Spain, where the company launched a new truck axle and transmission plant in Pamplona to supply the axle housing requirements for Eaton's French and Mexican operations. Eaton also teamed up with a Spanish company in a joint venture called Productos Eaton Livia S.A., which manufactured poppet valves, pushrods, and valve seat inserts for internal combustion engines and refrigeration compressors.[4]

In Italy, Eaton opened a new machine tool plant in Turin and purchased Italian manufacturer Elettrotecnica Padana S.r.l., which Eaton renamed Eaton Elpa S.p.A. The new subsidiary manufactured solenoid valves and coils, dispensers, microswitches, and thermostats for household appliances.[5]

Eaton's South American operations continued to prosper during this period. Eaton acquired a majority interest in Yale de Venezuela's lock and hardware manufacturing operation and opened a new automated foundry in Argentina, which suffered from a shortage of domestic foundries at the time.[6] In the 1960s, Eaton's international sales grew

Eaton continued to develop innovations such as this electronic igniter for gas appliances that reduced energy consumption by 30 percent.

from $30 million to $204 million annually, with nearly 50 overseas operations in 1969.[7] Between 1969 and 1970, Eaton's U.S. sales dropped, while international sales grew by 8 percent, constituting 27 percent of Eaton's sales and profits.[8]

### U.S. Endeavors

Domestically, Eaton sold off its floundering Marine Division in 1969, focusing instead on new expansion opportunities.[9] That year, Eaton acquired Cleveland-based Tinnerman Products Company. The subsidiary soon became the center of Eaton's Engineered Fasteners Division.

---

Eaton President William Mattie (far left) and CEO E. Mandell "Del" de Windt (second from left) are shown here on Wall Street with the Eaton Yale & Towne (EYT) stock symbol on the board in the background. *(Photo by Bob Cunningham Photography.)*

When Tinnerman was founded in 1870, it focused on manufacturing stoves and ranges. However, the company branched out in 1924 after the founder's son, A. H. Tinnerman, patented a spring fastening device called the "Speed Nut" that "revolutionized the assembly industry," according to the *Encyclopedia of Cleveland History*. The company soon began growing by leaps and bounds, and in 1940, Tinnerman abandoned its stove production business to focus solely on manufacturing industrial fasteners for use on factory assembly lines.[10]

In an effort to enter the lucrative aftermarket automobile components sector, Eaton acquired McQuay-Norris Manufacturing Company of St. Louis in 1969. McQuay-Norris, which manufactured engine and chassis components, had a large distribution network that seemed very promising. Unfortunately, Eaton soon faced legal challenges due to the acquisition.

In 1970, the Federal Trade Commission charged that the sale was a violation of the Clayton

Antitrust Act of 1914, which prohibited mergers and acquisitions that might negatively affect competition. The FTC sought to force Eaton to divest itself of McQuay-Norris and further ban Eaton from acquiring any company related to the automotive aftermarket for 10 years.[11] Denying fault, Eaton subsequently sold McQuay-Norris in 1976.[12]

Despite the setback, Eaton continued seeking prominent acquisitions, and in 1970, it purchased the Char-Lynn Company, a Minneapolis-based manufacturer of hydraulic motors for agriculture and industrial equipment. "Growth in the fluid power and controls field in the next 10 years is anticipated to be quite significant, and through the acquisition of Char-Lynn, we fully expect to become a significant factor in this market," Eaton CEO E. Mandell "Del" de Windt told the *Wall Street Journal*.[13]

According to Bill Butler, future Eaton chairman and CEO, "Char-Lynn was the real start of putting our hydraulics business on the map."[14]

### Struggling in a Down Economy

By 1969, Eaton employed more than 40,000 people in 92 plants across 13 countries. The company manufactured about 3,000 products for 50 industries and annual sales reached more than $1 billion. Eaton's truck operations had performed well during the 1960s, helping counteract losses in some of the company's less profitable divisions.[15]

Unfortunately, economic realities soon brought an end to that period of prosperity. "For Eaton, 1970 was a year of progress tempered by the relative adversity of a softened U.S. economy," stated Eaton's 1970 letter to shareholders.

Severe inflation, along with a dramatic slowdown in the U.S. economy, a rise in interest rates, and overall labor unrest in the industry took their toll on Eaton's bottom line. Inflation topped 6 percent by 1970. Trucking shipments were down, and the automotive industry fell into a slump as consumer spending plummeted due to the poor economy.[16] Eaton also experienced an increase of 6 percent in material costs and 5.5 percent in labor costs.[17]

The company faced additional challenges after a national Teamsters strike slowed truck ship-

Future Eaton Chairman and CEO Bill Butler served as Eaton's group vice president of industrial and security products during the late 1970s.

ments to and from Eaton's plants. The strike forced Eaton to temporarily shut down several plants in the United States. Eaton's operations in Cleveland, St. Louis, and Chicago suffered the most from the strike. Workers at the Tinnerman facility in Cleveland and an automotive spring plant in Ontario, Canada, also went on strike in 1970, forcing shutdowns that lasted up to three weeks.[18]

To combat the economic downturn, Eaton implemented an ambitious cost-cutting plan designed to reduce capital spending by more than $15 million. Some projects were postponed until the economy recovered. Plant operations were consolidated, production schedules were reduced in some plants, and Eaton was forced to institute a round of layoffs. Salaried and general office workers took 10 percent pay cuts.[19]

Despite the setbacks, Eaton did experience some success in the early 1970s. The company increased its plant capacity in Italy, Spain, and

South America. Eaton also acquired a 23 percent interest in Colorado-based Electron Corporation, whose operations included an iron foundry. The company continued expanding modestly, opening a new $4 million truck axle assembly plant in Henderson, Kentucky, and a tractor shovel plant in England.

### New Name, New Focus

As the economy continued to spiral downward, Eaton executives refocused their efforts and began instituting a plan to rebrand the company. The first major step involved changing the company's official name of Eaton Yale & Towne. Although that name was originally intended to increase Eaton's brand awareness, it did not have the anticipated effect. In fact, de Windt once recalled being introduced during a London meeting of international investment analysts as head of "Eaton Tale & Yawn."[20]

According to the 1970 Annual Report:

*Our name has for some time been a source of misunderstanding and confusion among our many publics. A corporate name today must function not only to project a clear and memorable identity, but also to endorse its brands and division names efficiently. [Our new name] had to be brief, easy to pronounce, and linguistically acceptable in all major countries due to our multi-national nature.*[21]

On April 21, 1971, the company was officially renamed Eaton Corporation. The new name was chosen for its straightforward simplicity.[22] That year, the company unveiled a new logo and launched an aggressive advertising campaign meant to increase Eaton's general public awareness. In an effort to raise its profile among everyday Americans, Eaton also sponsored a series of network documentaries related to poverty and social problems.[23]

Eaton's branding efforts came at a time of difficult challenges for the company. Sales remained flat for the early part of the decade, and ongoing labor unrest in the industry cost the company $4 million in the first half of 1971 alone. At the same time, the global economy continued to plummet and the United States was beset by both stagnant

In 1971, Eaton Yale & Towne became Eaton Corporation. The Eaton name and its new logo were prominently displayed at the Southfield, Michigan, research center.

growth and inflation. "Our biggest problem at the moment is inflation," de Windt told the *Wall Street Journal*, noting that the rate was much higher than the company had anticipated.[24]

To compound the problem, in 1971, the Nixon administration implemented strict wage and price controls on an array of industries, preventing Eaton from raising prices to match the increase in costs for materials and labor. Intended to slow the pace of inflation, the unpopular price controls continued for three more years despite the fact that they did little to stop the skyrocketing inflation.[25] According to de Windt, the controls "had a very depressing effect on our ability to adjust prices to meet the increased costs and put a very definite squeeze on our profit margins."[26]

As it struggled with an exceedingly difficult business climate in the United States, Eaton maintained a strong focus on its international operations. The company began investigating new foreign acquisitions, especially in Eastern European countries such as Yugoslavia. Vice President and General Counsel Melvin Arnold, who would go on to become executive vice president of law and corporate relations, considered Yugoslavia the "doorway to many future opportunities."[27] Eaton expanded to Yugoslavia in 1972, forming the first joint venture of a U.S. company in Eastern Europe by acquiring a minority interest in the Rudi Cajavec Company.[28]

By 1973, Western Europe manufactured more passenger cars than the United States. That year, Eaton acquired the Holzer Group of West Germany, a $30 million company with facilities in Germany and Italy that manufactured appliance and automotive controls. Eaton also acquired Transport Equipment Ltd., a transmission manufacturer based in the United Kingdom, and also purchased 80 percent of Milan, Italy–based Nova Werke S.p.A., which specialized in manufacturing components such as pistons, piston rings, and piston sleeve assemblies.[29]

Eaton's passenger car components manufacturing business continued to thrive in Brazil, which had produced upwards of half a million

cars by 1973. Eaton's engine component operations in that country remained a bright spot, with positive sales numbers that led the company to manufacture additional products in Brazil, such as hydraulic lifters and rocker arms.[30]

In the United States, Eaton opened an axle plant in Glasgow, Kentucky, that was the largest single capital investment in the company's history up to that point. Eaton also began construction on an axle housing plant in Humboldt, Tennessee, and expanded its transmission plants in Iowa, Michigan, and Tennessee.[31]

Eaton continued developing innovative new technology, including two heavy-duty truck transmission lines designed to cut down on gear damage. Eaton also expanded the reach of its popular Roadranger twin countershaft transmission, with new versions tailored to short-wheelbase tractors and high-horsepower engines. By 1973, the Brake Division developed a truck skid-control system, just in time to benefit from the heightened federal standards for truck braking that went into effect that year. Eaton soon opened a new plant devoted to the skid-control brakes in Sanford, North Carolina.[32] According to the *New York Times*, the company's newly developed antilock brakes were equipped with computerized electrical components that nearly halved stopping distances while preventing skidding and jackknifing, adding that the brakes "prevent wheels from locking in panic stops by automatically releasing and reapplying the brakes in a staccato fashion until the truck comes to a complete halt. The equipment presumably allows much heavier, more powerful brakes on trucks than were formerly practical."[33]

Eaton continued to focus on innovative technology, announcing a new line of heavy-duty hydrostatic transmissions. Previously, Eaton's hydrostatic transmissions were only available for lower-horsepower vehicles such as farm machinery. In addition, Eaton opened a new plant in Spencer, Iowa, that manufactured complete fluid power systems suited for any vehicle requiring varying drive speed ratios and maneuverability.[34] The company also developed a new mechanical

Del de Windt successfully led the company for 17 years.

transmission for heavy-duty trucks. Known as the Eaton Snapper, it was capable of shifting automatically between speeds within a selected gear.[35] The Fluid Power Division, thanks in part to its acquisition of Char-Lynn, also introduced two new series of hydraulic motors and a revised version of the Orbitrol, a hydraulic power steering device.[36] Eaton also attempted to diversify into the consumer marketplace, debuting 16 auto service centers in Houston and Dallas as part of a pilot program. Unfortunately, the centers did not perform as well as anticipated, and Eaton ultimately returned its focus to the manufacturing sector.[37]

Venturing into the consumer market for the first time, Eaton opened a line of auto service centers in Texas in 1973. However, the planned expansion never materialized and Eaton returned its focus to the manufacturing sector.

## Struggling Through a Recession

After the lifting of price controls in 1974, Eaton was once again able to successfully renegotiate prices with its customers. Across the country, Eaton's customers anticipated an upswing and began back-ordering countless components to assure access to supplies. To keep up with the skyrocketing demand, Eaton operated its transmission plants around the clock while struggling to allocate its available product inventories to its customers. By late 1974, however, the anticipated economic recovery had never materialized, and orders dwindled, leaving Eaton overburdened with excess inventory and shrinking profit margins.[38]

At the end of the year, the economic outlook remained grim, with many analysts predicting a difficult period of continued recession and inflation. Eaton was forced to institute layoffs and

cut back on work shifts.[39] However, these cuts were only a prelude to the difficult economic realities Eaton would continue to face in 1975. That year, sales dropped 11 percent and plants began operating at a drastically reduced 40 percent to 70 percent of capacity. Earnings fell 48 percent. The recession crippled the U.S. economy, caused in part by an oil embargo in 1973 that had finally caught up with the U.S. capital goods sector.

Eaton's truck, car, and materials handling businesses all suffered declines. Especially hard-hit were Eaton's light truck and lock and hardware business segments. According to the 1975 Annual Report:

*Nineteen seventy-five was a difficult year. We were affected by a greatly curtailed customer demand, adverse international currency devaluations, continued inflation, cost increases, and, as a result, lower sales and profits.*[40]

By the 1970s, Eaton had become the leading manufacturer of truck axles, transmissions, and brakes.

Inset: An evocative photo of the forging of a truck axle gear graced the cover of Eaton's 1979 Annual Report.

In an attempt to counteract the downturn, the company formed the Operations Cost Reduction Committee, which ultimately helped the company save nearly $31 million. Eaton cut costs and divested itself of underperforming divisions. The company laid off nearly 7,000 employees worldwide, reducing its workforce by approximately 13 percent. The company also sold its watercooler product manufacturing line in Lanark, Illinois, and its European dispenser operation. In all, Eaton slashed its costs by $100 million.

More than 5,000 employees contributed their own money-saving ideas for the company, many of which were implemented by Eaton. Other cost-saving measures included substituting materials and implementing design and manufacturing changes. Executives also found ways to trim office expenses by 15 percent per year.[41]

Despite the many setbacks, Eaton continued pressing ahead with ambitious research and development projects. Innovations introduced that year included a fuel-saving six-speed transmission, along with a new series of axles designed for trucks weighing more than 23,000 pounds. By

This photo shows Eaton's Southfield, Michigan, research center in the early 1970s, after the completion of a $5.5 million expansion. The addition included new laboratories for electronic parts work, materials handling, instrumentation, and safety research.

that point, Eaton was manufacturing the most complete line of axles for heavy-duty trucks in the country. The company expanded its axle manufacturing capacity with a new plant in Humboldt, Tennessee, giving Eaton the capacity to produce entire axles, including all components and housings, entirely in the United States.[42] Eaton's cruise control, already claiming 15 percent of the market, also experienced newfound momentum with the introduction of a national speed limit of 55 mph.[43]

However, the 1975 sales decline still cut deeply. Eaton's truck, car, and materials handling businesses all fell simultaneously. Materials handling, which hadn't performed as well as expected for years, lost approximately $12 million. Nearly all of the businesses gained as part of the Yale & Towne acquisition in 1963 were underperforming, dragging down Eaton's bottom line in the process.

The time for change had come, and de Windt brought together Eaton's executive team to decide on a new direction.[44] Under the plan, Eaton began acquiring cutting-edge technology businesses with abundant growth potential.[45] According to internal documents, Eaton's new direction aimed to "establish Eaton's presence in selected new markets, [achieving] a mix of businesses which will provide increased average growth in earnings per share, add businesses that would lessen Eaton's vulnerability to short-term changes in the world economy, and supplement Eaton's professional skills in management, marketing, engineering, and manufacturing."[46]

Eaton embarked on a two-year study to identify possible merger and acquisition candidates. The criteria for acquisition targets included a primary focus on technology, a strong position in the marketplace, and an international base similar to Eaton's.[47]

## Eaton Rebounds

In 1976, Eaton sold off its interests in precision rubber products and automatic door openers, as well as its Brazilian industrial drives segment. The company also sought a buyer for its lock, hardware, and security products business unit, ultimately selling that unit to the Scovill Manufacturing Company of Waterbury, Connecticut, in February 1978, for $56 million. "Effective strategic planning demands that we constantly evaluate our current businesses and their performance against planned objectives," stated the 1977 letter to shareholders. "Those which after a reasonable time do not meet long-term objectives become candidates for phase-out and divesture."[48]

A rebounding U.S. economy also helped propel Eaton forward. Passenger car sales increased 25 percent from 1975 to 1976, and trucks surpassed even that, gaining 35 percent.[49] By the following year, a leaner Eaton was on track to reach the $2 billion sales mark. Although overseas operations were down, Eaton vowed to keep investing in them to "achieve the strong potential of these important markets," according to its 1977 Annual Report.[50]

As Eaton recovered from the economic setbacks, the company continued divesting itself of

Eaton's strong focus on research and development continued to help the company persevere during difficult economic climates.

businesses that were no longer in line with its core manufacturing priorities. In 1979, the Gear Division in Richmond, Indiana, was sold for $8 million. Eaton also divested itself of the Dispenser Division in Cleveland, Ohio, and a Forge Division plant in West Allis, Wisconsin.[51]

As the company rebounded in the late 1970s, Eaton made important inroads overseas. For the first time, Eaton entered the engine valve market in Japan, signing a licensing agreement with Nittan Valve Co.[52] In Hungary, Eaton negotiated a 10-year agreement with RABA Hungarian Railway Carriage and Machine Works that would market RABA-designed truck components in Europe and North America. The deal provided both companies with important international contacts, and RABA

# FRANK R. BACON

IN 1892, FOLLOWING THE DEATH of his mother, Frank R. Bacon left Princeton University for Milwaukee, Wisconsin, to work with his father at E. P. Bacon & Company. However, he retained his passion for mechanical engineering and saw promise in the growing demand for electrical equipment. Intrigued by a no-voltage release starting box for motors, he formed a partnership with inventor Lucius T. Gibbs.

After Gibbs received a patent on the device, the two founded American Rheostat Company in Milwaukee. The starting box was their first product, and it happened to be very similar to one manufactured by the Chicago company Cutler-Hammer. Unfortunately, the starter Gibbs developed had several flaws. Bacon bought out the partnership and redeveloped the starter, receiving a new patent for the device.

Although the starter sold well, American Rheostat found itself in a legal battle with Cutler-Hammer, each claiming to own the rights to the device. A third company, Western Electric, soon became involved in the protracted legal battle. In the meantime, Cutler-Hammer cofounder Edward West Hammer sold his interest in the company to his partner Harry Henderson Cutler. Sensing the best opportunity to end the legal stalemate, in 1897, Bacon acquired Cutler-Hammer. The newly merged company was known as Cutler-Hammer because of its greater name recognition.[1]

However, the company found itself in the midst of a severe economic recession. Business slowed to a trickle, and the number of employees shrank from 75 to 5. However, Bacon refused to give up,

focusing his efforts on diversification. By 1899, Bacon's efforts had proved successful, and the company began to expand once again. According to *Cutler-Hammer: 75 Year Perspective on the Future*:

> *[Bacon] learned a lesson from the American Rheostat Co. It had had only one product, and when that one product was in trouble, the whole company had floundered. Bacon was determined never to be caught without a product which could take over from a failing one. He spurred new product development.*[2]

Bacon remained dedicated to encouraging research and development within the company, while promoting a strong emphasis on customer service and support. Under his leadership, the company developed a wide array of products, and sales skyrocketed from $193,000 in 1900 to $12 million in 1920.[3]

would go on to become a major customer of Eaton's truck transmissions.[53]

Eaton also made several important acquisitions during this time that complemented the company's automotive and truck component manufacturing business, most notably Cutler-Hammer Inc. and its defense electronics subsidiary, Airborne Instruments Laboratory (AIL), in 1978. This landmark acquisition would go on to form the foundation of Eaton's electrical business. Cutler-Hammer, an 86-year-old company based in Milwaukee, specialized in manufacturing industrial controls and power distribution electrical equipment for industrial and commercial markets, specialty electrical controls for commercial and aerospace applications, equipment for defense applications, and semiconductor components. AIL developed the ALQ-161 advanced radar countermeasures system for Rockwell's B-1B bomber. Cutler-Hammer's expertise was so renowned that NASA selected the company to build the landing system for the Space Shuttle. Assembly lines across the world featured Cutler-Hammer controls, with products ranging from starters to computer control systems. Cutler-Hammer also developed a broad array of semiconductor manufacturing and test equipment.

Above: Airborne Instruments Laboratory (AIL) developed an advanced radar countermeasures system for the B-1B bomber. *(Photo courtesy U.S. Department of Defense.)*

Below: NASA selected Cutler-Hammer to build the landing system for the Space Shuttle program. Here, the Space Shuttle *Columbia* is shown returning to Earth after its first orbital mission. *(Photo courtesy NASA.)*

# CUTLER-HAMMER

THE 1978 ACQUISITION OF Cutler-Hammer has proved key to Eaton's strong growth in the electrical industry in the past three decades. Cutler-Hammer was founded in Chicago in 1892 by a partnership between inventor Harry Henderson Cutler, who amassed a lifetime total of 73 patents for electric control devices, and his business partner Edward West Hammer. It specialized in electric starters, speed regulators, and field rheostats.

In 1897, Cutler-Hammer was purchased by American Rheostat, a Milwaukee-based competitor also founded in 1892. The two companies had similar patents on a no-voltage release starting box for motors, and had initiated court actions against each other before the deal. Under the agreement, American Rheostat acquired the plant and all rights for Cutler-Hammer, but agreed to continue operating under the Cutler-Hammer name, which enjoyed wider brand recognition. American Rheostat's Frank R. Bacon became chairman and

75 Year Perspective on the Future

president of the consolidated firm, with Cutler serving as chief engineer.

The company grew steadily, from 400 employees in 1904, to 3,400 by 1940. In 1954, Cutler-Hammer purchased Airborne Instruments Laboratory (AIL), an innovative aerospace company that was struggling financially. Founded in 1940 by a group of MIT engineers at Quonset Point (Rhode Island) Naval Air Station during World War II, AIL developed electronic

countermeasures and jamming devices to defend against German radio-commanded missiles.

After the war, AIL engineers teamed up with scientists from Harvard's Radio Research Lab and became officially incorporated. The company planned to adapt the technology it had developed for wartime navigation and signaling devices to commercial airlines. By the time of the Cutler-Hammer purchase, AIL had 900 employees.[1]

Cutler-Hammer expanded rapidly in the 1960s, growing from a staff of 7,000 in 1960, to 11,500 by 1966. In 1977, Cutler-Hammer had sales of $517 million with an income of $24 million. The $376 million Cutler-Hammer acquisition allowed Eaton to expand into new fields in electronic technology, with an emphasis on defense electronics for the aviation industry.[2]

Above: Cutler-Hammer celebrated its 75th anniversary in 1967.

Right: With a strong focus on innovation, Cutler-Hammer developed many new technologies, including an experimental electronic control for printing presses, pictured here in 1943.

The acquisition proved instrumental in helping Eaton achieve record sales in 1979. Eaton hit $3 billion in annual sales that year, and advanced 20 places, from 121 to 101, in the FORTUNE® 500 list of the largest industrial companies.[54] James R. Stover, vice chairman of the board, was named chief operating officer.

Eaton also gained a new chief financial officer, Stephen Hardis. In a 1979 *Wall Street Journal* article, Hardis was commended for having the foresight to arrange $350 million in bank loans just

James R. Stover, who started out as a patent attorney at Eaton, became chief operating officer in 1979. He would go on to become chairman and CEO in 1986.

before the Federal Reserve tightened credit regulations.[55] The loan would give Eaton flexibility in its expansion and acquisition strategies in the new decade—a time of uncertainty marked by the Iranian hostage crisis, stagflation, and a deep recession.

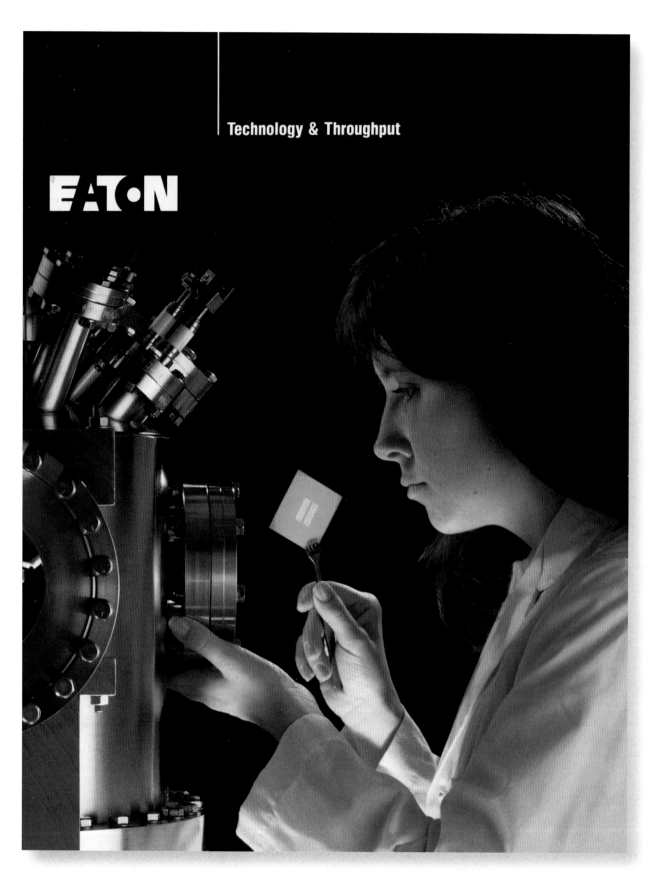

**Technology & Throughput**

This 1987 Eaton booklet emphasized the company's technological advancements.

## CHAPTER EIGHT

# BRIGHTER PROSPECTS
## 1980 – 1991

*It is evident that our economy is dealing with some fundamental problems,
and that changes of a basic and structural nature are taking place.*

—1981 Annual Report[1]

BY THE EARLY 1980s, IN THE WAKE OF the oil and energy crisis of the previous decade, a severe recession struck the United States. Nearly every industry was affected, and North American automobile production plummeted to a 20-year low.[2] According to Eaton's 1980 Annual Report, the depressed state of the economy, and the auto industry in particular, remained an ongoing worry.[3] Fortunately, Eaton had successfully focused on diversifying its operations in the previous decades, and by 1981, the passenger car market accounted for less than 10 percent of Eaton's sales, with truck components accounting for 31 percent of the business. Eaton had also streamlined its operations, organizing the company into three groups: Electronic and Electrical, Vehicle Components, and Materials Handling.[4]

In a 1981 article emphasizing Eaton's diversification efforts, *BusinessWeek* praised Eaton CEO E. Mandell "Del" de Windt for "emphasizing truck parts while reducing dependence on more consistently depressed auto parts." The article predicted that, despite a slowdown in profits, Eaton would soon be in a better position than its competitors, thanks to a long-range diversification plan that had included the purchase of Cutler-Hammer, as well as

several important acquisitions in the fields of hydraulics, semiconductors, and factory automation.[5]

Executives at the company remained optimistic about the high potential for growth in the emerging semiconductor industry, and Eaton acquired Lorlin Industries of Danbury, Connecticut, and Optimetrix Corporation of Mountain View, California.[6] Analysts predicted Eaton's earnings would more than double by 1983. "We purchased all our 777,200 Eaton shares in the last year [based] on the thesis that diversification has changed the company," announced Kenneth J. Greiner, an analyst with the College Retirement Equities Fund (CREF).[7]

However, Eaton also recognized that it needed to make further changes. "It is evident that our economy is dealing with some fundamental problems, and that changes of a basic and structural nature are taking place," noted the company's 1981 Annual Report.[8] With more competition among vendors in a global marketplace, manufacturers

The viscous converter clutch, which offered smoother shifting and better fuel economy, was first offered for the 1984 Cadillac DeVille.

were pressured to lower production costs and finance costly research and development efforts that manufacturers had previously performed in-house.[9]

Even as Eaton continued to gain market share, truck component sales had fallen exceptionally low from 1979 to 1981, due to a depressed market that had a detrimental effect on Eaton's new lines of heavy-duty axles and lightweight brakes, as well as truck transmissions, which were historically Eaton's most profitable truck components. However, new military truck contracts helped Eaton weather the storm.[10] In an effort to cut back on production costs, Eaton wrote off $100 million of obsolete plants and equipment from 1978 to 1981, and spent $125 million to increase productivity at its remaining plants. Another $50 million was invested in product and market research.[11]

U.S. exports overall suffered as the dollar rose in the early 1980s. To survive the financial troubles of an unstable economic climate, the company also changed its capital structure. Eaton doubled its debt maturity to more than 12 years and increased its credit lines to more than $500 million.[12]

The company also cut its workforce by about 13 percent, from a high of 58,000 in 1978, to just over 50,000 in 1980. "It is painful to have parted with approximately 7,400 loyal Eaton employees at all levels," company leaders lamented. "But the result is the lean and more productive operation that current economic realities require."[13]

Unfortunately, the situation continued to deteriorate. In 1982, Eaton suffered its first annual loss in 50 years, since the height of the Great Depression. Domestic car sales fell to 30-year lows and prospects dimmed in all of Eaton's markets, with the exception of defense electronics. Heavy-duty truck production plummeted, down 40 percent from 1979. Also that year, Eaton suffered from lagging sales in its lift truck and forestry equipment businesses.[14] To turn things around, the company decided to implement a three-part course of action known as "Operation Shrink": resolve problems in the perennially struggling Lift Truck and Forestry Division businesses, cut back further on production costs, and cut dividend payments nearly in half.[15]

"At the time, it was very dramatic," said Stephen Hardis, who became chief financial officer in 1979 and would go on to serve as Eaton chairman and CEO. "It was relatively unprecedented in our kind of industrial business. The result was that when the recovery started in 1983—but really got going in 1984—we made more money than we had ever made, and we picked up competitive advantage in our businesses."[16]

With growth slowing in the truck market and 25 percent of the automobile market shifted to overseas companies, "it would be foolhardy to wait passively for a recovery to come and solve our problems," noted the company's 1982 letter to shareholders.[17]

By early 1983, Eaton was aggressively implementing Operation Shrink. It had sold its Canadian-based forestry equipment business and divested 81 percent of the lift truck business to German, British, and Japanese buyers.[18] Eaton also spent $200 million to close plants, and was forced to cut its dividend payout by more than 50 percent. The

Stephen Hardis served as Eaton's chief financial officer during the 1980s.

economic downturn forced the company to lay off more workers and close nine plants in total—seven in the Midwest, one in Kentucky, and one in Canada. All told, approximately 22,000 Eaton employees lost their jobs during the five-year down-sizing period.[19]

It was an extremely challenging time for the company. According to the 1983 letter to share-holders, "There is ... still a very strong sense of dis-tress concerning the 22,000 Eaton employees who are no longer with the company. This loss was by far the most wrenching and painful part of reshap-ing Eaton. It was necessary, but it will be a long time before the memory of it fades."

Thomas O'Boyle, who led the company's trans-mission business at the time, recalled the difficult transition: "We let a lot of very, very good people go. A lot of those people went right back into the same industry, and we ended up working with them in different areas with different customers."[20]

The company did everything it could to limit the layoffs, offering employees jobs at other locations whenever possible. "Some employees relocated," re-called future Senior Vice President of Hydraulics and Automotive Controls Bob McCloskey, a plant manager in Cleveland at the time. "Others were offered jobs, [but] they decided not to relocate."[21]

Despite the difficulties, future Chairman and CEO Stephen Hardis recalled the loyalty and motivation of Eaton employees, "There's a commit-ment to the company that's extraordinary. It's a cyclical business, and there are layoffs. People come back in large part because they own a sense of pride in working here, and that's something that each leader was fortunate enough to inherit and build on."[22]

## A New Future

Eaton persevered by maintaining a strict focus on its future prospects, increasing research spending from $10 million to $100 million, and opening an advanced electronics research facility in Milwaukee and an electronics sensor plant in Athens, Georgia.[23] By 1983, markets had begun to turn around as Eaton returned to profitabil-ity. The company had significantly streamlined its operations, with 40,000 employees and 140 facilities in 16 countries.[24] The company also reaffirmed its commitment to the city of Cleveland, relocating its 100 Erieview headquarters to the nearby Eaton Center at 1111 Superior Avenue in 1984.[25]

"Despite some initial pains, Eaton Corporation should emerge better off from its sweeping decision to cut the lifeline to some of its long-suffering busi-nesses," stated a 1983 article in *Automotive News*.[26]

Goldman Sachs analyst Patrick K. Fricke said Eaton had been right to divest itself of its lift trucks and forestry business, calling it "a great drag on the company. It has $300 million worth of assets and isn't earning anything."[27]

Despite the recession, Eaton was optimistic about the long-term viability of truck components. The company had been steadily investing in its truck lines over the years, updating its tried-and-true products and introducing others. From the late 1970s to early 1980s, it quadrupled research and development facilities and more than doubled product-development spending in this area.[28]

In 1980, Eaton invested in new headquar-ters and research facilities in Galesburg, Michigan, for the Transmissions and Brake divisions, and spent $59 million in capital projects for truck components. According to the 1980 Annual Report, "The full and vigorous recovery of the truck indus-try is a certainty."

In 1981, most of Eaton's truck components plants were less than 10 years old. "These facilities, strategically located worldwide and among the most sophisticated anywhere, are designed to operate at high levels of efficiency, yielding greater productiv-ity," stated the Annual Report that year.[29]

Also in 1981, Eaton introduced its first air-disc brake for heavy-duty trucks, and came out with a line of highway axles and all-wheel drive axle sys-tems, including front-steer drive axles. Additionally, the company landed $100 million in contracts for drive axles and brakes on three types of heavy-duty U.S. Army vehicles.[30]

Eaton continued to focus on potential high-growth market segments, including hydraulic power transmissions for the off-highway market, particu-larly hydrostatic transmissions. At the time, Eaton was the second-largest manufacturer of hydrosta-tic transmissions in North America.[31] In 1981, Eaton invested $20 million in redesigning its line of Fuller transmissions for heavy trucks.

# DIVERSIFICATION

THROUGHOUT ITS HISTORY, EATON has been a forward-thinking company, committed to a long-term strategy of growth through innovation and diversification ever since the days of J. O. Eaton. His vision and talent helped Eaton become a true corporate success with real staying power.

In Eaton's early days, diversification often meant acquiring companies that manufactured vehicle components complementary to Eaton's offerings or that owned valuable patents that would expand Eaton's existing product lines. Eaton devoted its efforts to improving production and making newly acquired divisions more profitable. The company's executives often demonstrated a prescient ability to determine which acquisitions would benefit the company the most in the long run. Perfection Spring & Stamping Corporation was one of the first—a healthy operation specializing in manufacturing leaf springs for car chassis, with a plant located near Eaton's operation in Cleveland. As bumpers were just beginning to become a standard feature on new car models, Eaton acquired the country's first bumper manufacturer and quickly installed new machinery designed to streamline and automate the manufacturing process. According to longtime Eaton board member John Miller, "If you go back to the origins of the company, the company has had a history over the years of continuously reinventing itself as circumstances dictated. They've been very successful in that regard, and they continue along those lines today."[1]

In 1982, Eaton introduced the Twin Splitter, a new truck gearbox designed to address the increasing demand for shorter cargo trips combined with rail and waterway transport. The Twin Splitter was designed for short-distance urban transport requiring frequent manual shifting, especially in mountainous terrain.[32] After three years of design and testing, in 1983 Eaton introduced The Beast, a truck axle with a previously unheard-of 600,000-mile warranty. It was designed for a new market: trucks able to haul multiple trailers. Also that year, the company debuted an automobile engine supercharger with improved acceleration and fuel economy and a viscous converter clutch for the 1984 Cadillac DeVille that eliminated the typical spring clutch engaging and disengaging. Car buyers were again in the market for larger vehicles, but these cars still had to meet new fuel economy requirements.[33]

Eaton built the heavy-duty axles used on the U.S. Army's Heavy Expanded Mobility Tactical Trucks (HEMTTs), vehicles designed for use in the roughest terrain.

During the Great Depression, Eaton entered what would become a lucrative business manufacturing sodium-cooled valves for military aircraft by acquiring Wilcox-Rich, a formidable company struggling during a time of economic upheavals. Smart acquisitions during that period allowed the company to emerge triumphant following the Depression and World War II.

In the 1950s, Eaton acquired Fuller Manufacturing Company, a manufacturer of truck transmissions. This was an especially smart move because diversifying into this area allowed Eaton to offer medium- and heavy-duty truck transmissions alongside its axles. Decade after decade, the acquisition has continued to pay off.

Beginning in the 1960s, Eaton began acquiring companies with a global reach in an effort to build its international reputation, a strategy Chairman and CEO Del de Windt considered key to the company's future. Eaton invested in truck-axle companies in Italy and the United Kingdom, and launched operations in South America.

By the late 1970s, with the acquisition of Cutler-Hammer, Eaton gained important defense contracts and entered the lucrative electrical controls business. Eaton's acquisition skills have only improved over time, as evidenced by later acquisitions in the 21st century, such as the Westinghouse Distribution and Control Business Unit, Moeller, and Phoenixtec. According to Ted Wheeler, senior vice president and research analyst at Buckingham Research Group, "I think Eaton really recognized their core strengths in the automotive and truck markets were very valuable but had certain limits in terms of growth. And so they've really been developing core strengths in all of their industrial markets. The change has been to develop meaningful value-added market positions in industries somewhat related to the vehicle business in terms of type of customer, but unrelated in terms of the ultimate buyer—and electrical and fluid power are the horses on that score now."[2]

*Barron's* magazine praised Eaton's successful turnaround:

> *Eaton emerged from the recession a leaner, meaner manufacturer of its most profitable products: medium- and heavy-duty truck axles, five-speed manual transmissions, valves, brakes, and some passenger car and off-road vehicle parts.*[34]

In the heavy-duty trucks market, Eaton announced its plan to introduce a fully automatic transmission within the next 10 years. According to Robert Gillison, president of Eaton's Truck Components Group, "The technology for such a gearbox, relying heavily on electronics, exists today, [but Eaton] was waiting for the truck market to catch up."[35]

Meanwhile, the company had two new generations of Eaton truck transmissions ready to go—a semi-automated transmission for both the military and commercial markets, and an automatic Roadranger transmission for long-haul trucks. Both debuted in Europe before being introduced in the United States.[36]

Although in the past it had focused mainly on heavy-duty trucks, Eaton began to see potential in the medium-duty transmission market. Between 1980 and 1986, demand for medium-duty trucks grew 72 percent.[37]

The company signed a deal with Ford to produce medium-duty transmissions for the Ford Cargo, a cab-over-engine freight truck. It also partnered with Iveco, a major European truck producer, to develop a medium-duty truck transmission for the European market.[38]

In 1987, Eaton became a major medium-duty truck transmission supplier after it entered into a partnership with Clark Equipment Company. Under the terms of the agreement, Eaton would redesign Clark's CL Series 5-speed transmissions, producing the renamed Mid-Range line alongside Eaton's own FS Series 5-speed and 6-speed transmissions at its São Paulo plant. The contract broadly expanded Eaton's customer base to include companies such as General Motors.[39]

In May 1988, Eaton created a Drivetrain Systems Division that backed up its commitment to truck components. According to the 1988

Annual Report, "We expect to be the only company that will be able to offer a complete system integration to the truck manufacturers—from flywheels to wheels."[40]

Also that year, Eaton entered a joint venture with French vehicle component maker Valeo to manufacture and market truck clutches in the United States. The partnership added clutches to Eaton's line of transmissions and axles, while allowing Valeo to break into the U.S. truck market.[41] Unfortunately,

the joint venture ultimately proved unsuccessful and had to be dissolved.

In 1989, after 16 months of intense testing, Eaton began supplying components for Hyundai's new 20-ton dump truck.[42] The company also continued to expand internationally, with Korea becoming one of the fastest-growing markets for Eaton's truck components. Truck component sales skyrocketed to $30 million by 1990.

By the end of the decade, Eaton had regained its footing in the heavy-duty truck components manufacturing sector. Medium-duty business also flourished, although competitors began to challenge Eaton's position in the heavy-duty transmission market. Since transmission designs were not difficult to replicate, Eaton's competitors contacted the company's customers and claimed to offer the same product. However, Eaton's competitors charged up to 20 percent less.[43]

Rather than cut prices, Eaton decided to improve the company's core product line. The newly improved transmission line, called Concept 2000, was launched in 1990.[44]

## Defense and Divestiture

As Eaton's vehicle components markets struggled in the early 1980s, its government defense and nondefense electronics business continued to expand. Sales in that segment would more than quadruple by the end of the decade.[45]

Eaton's advanced electronics products and systems included the microwave landing and communications systems for America's first Space Shuttle, vessel traffic control systems for the Suez Canal, and air traffic control systems for a dozen countries, including Canada, Yugoslavia, and China.[46] Sales in the company's Aerospace and Defense Systems Division rose to $201 million in 1981.[47]

A few years before Eaton acquired Cutler-Hammer, the latter company successfully bid on a government contract for the B-1B bomber. The Air Force's new long-range strategic bomber was

A microprocessor controlled Eaton's Automated Mechanical Transmission (AMT), which was designed for the heavy-duty truck market and introduced in the late 1980s.

Eaton developed the microwave landing system for the Space Shuttle *Columbia*, which provided autopilot guidance up to eight miles from the shuttle's landing target.

Eaton's largest single contract up to that point.[48] The contract brought more than $1 billion in sales during the next decade. Eaton supplied the anti-radar equipment to intercept and jam signals from enemy aircraft as well as keep the plane from being detected during a secret mission.[49] In addition, beginning in 1981, Eaton supplied $37 million in electronic countermeasures systems for the U.S. Navy's EA-6B and the Air Force's EF-111 aircraft.[50] The company also worked on developing systems for *Voyager 2* and the Space Shuttle *Columbia*. Astronaut Neil Armstrong joined Eaton's board of directors on April 22, 1981.

Eaton continued making scientific progress and landed several new contracts, expanding its specialties to include electronic countermeasures for defense aircraft, traffic control systems for airports and waterways, and low noise amplifiers that allowed astronomers to monitor sounds from outer space.

In 1982, despite the lingering recession, Eaton's defense electronics business grew 50 percent in volume. Long-term contracts for the B-1B bomber held by Eaton's Airborne Instruments Laboratory (AIL) subsidiary, acquired as part of the Cutler-Hammer acquisition, were the main reason for this growth, along with contracts for the initial development phase of a radar detection system for the U.S. Navy's P-3C Orion antisubmarine aircraft, and scientific studies, including testing an ultra low frequency (ULF) communications system for submarines.[51]

By 1985, Eaton's Aerospace and Defense Systems Division revenues rose to more than four times what they had been in 1981. Those revenues were at $979 million, much of that a direct result of the B-1B project, while at least $350 million came from new, unrelated contracts.[52] *Forbes* magazine praised the division as "Eaton's biggest success so far on the new frontier," noting the cyclical nature of the semiconductor industry.

According to an analyst at the time, "[Eaton's] earnings used to drop 50 percent, 60 percent,

even 90 percent from peak to trough of an economic cycle. Now they stand a pretty good chance of mitigating the decline to 15 percent to 20 percent in a moderate downturn."[53]

The first of the contracted 100 B-1Bs—which included two tons of electronic countermeasure equipment—was delivered to the Air Force in 1985. Unfortunately, according to the company's 1986 Annual Report, the B-1B project, along with Eaton's defensive avionics system, "came under public scrutiny for a variety of problems, including performance."

Eaton worked tirelessly with the Air Force to complete the project satisfactorily.[54] Performance quickly improved on the B-1B bomber.

Unfortunately, in June 1988, Eaton suffered a significant blow when the Air Force canceled its $153 million contract for EF-111 warplanes. An article in the *Wall Street Journal* said the Air Force canceled the contract "after Eaton's AIL unit in Deer Park, New York, fell behind in delivering the equipment, which is vital to evading enemy air defenses."

By 1989, the government's withheld payments on the B-1B project decreased from $235 million to $159 million. Once the performance issues related to the B-1B were resolved, Eaton announced its intention to sell off its defense electronics business. The business, stated the company's 1989 Annual Report, required substantial expansion to succeed over the long term, and Eaton was "unwilling to make the investments needed for that growth, given the better opportunities in our commercial businesses. Simply put, we must get bigger in defense electronics or get out, and we think our resources are better applied in other businesses."[55]

Despite the lingering recession, Eaton's defense electronics business continued to grow, due in large part to long-term contracts such as the initial development phase of a radar detection system for the U.S. Navy's P-3C Orion antisubmarine aircraft. *(Photo courtesy U.S. Department of Defense.)*

An article in *Aviation Week & Space Technology* called the announcement "a major exit from the device electronics market." Eaton Chairman and CEO James Stover, quoted in the article, said that "the special procedures required for defense electronics contractors are hard to justify, except with the economies of scale permitted by very large commitments in the defense contract arena. We have concluded that our choice is either to invest in a very substantial expansion of our defense electronics operations or exit this business."[56]

Six months later, B-1B manufacturer Rockwell International agreed to buy AIL.[57] However, the agreement fell through, and Eaton took AIL off the market for several years and ran it as a separate subsidiary. In 1989, Signet Technology Corporation of Boston bought the Microwave

In the 1980s, Eaton supplied the defensive countermeasures electronics system for the Air Force's B–1B bomber.

Products Division, the remainder of Eaton's defense electronics business.[58]

Eaton has continued to work with the government, especially in the electrical and aerospace sectors. According to John Miller, a longtime member of Eaton's board of directors, "The lesson learned is that there's a different culture that's required to deal with ... the Defense Department as a customer."[59]

## Moving Forward

During the mid-1980s, the company's financial situation began to improve. By 1984, earnings rose to $254 million, up 173 percent from the previous year. Sales had risen 31 percent to $3.5 billion, with 51.2 percent of those sales coming from the electric and electronics sector. Eaton also acquired Bunker–Ramo Electronics Systems, which was added to the company's Defense Systems business, and Master Specialties Company, a California maker of aircraft and commercial controls.[60]

A year later, Eaton increased dividends, expanded the common share repurchase program, and issued share purchase rights to protect shareholders from unsolicited takeover attempts. It also jumped to No. 103 in the FORTUNE® 500.[61]

In 1986, after 17 years as CEO and 45 years with Eaton, Del de Windt retired at the age of 65. He was succeeded by James R. Stover as chairman and CEO. Future CEO Sandy Cutler, one of Eaton's foremost young operating managers, was named the new president of the Industrial Group.[62]

That year, Eaton acquired The Singer Company's Controls Division, which manufactured electronic and electromechanical control devices for automotive and appliance manufacturers. Eaton also purchased Consolidated Controls Corporation, which manufactured transducers, pressure switches, actuators, and power control systems for the aerospace, marine, and defense industries. This brought the number of companies Eaton had acquired in the previous eight years to 17.[63]

In 1987, Eaton was named to the FORTUNE® 100 for the first time.[64] The company embarked on several joint ventures that year, including a venture with Korea's Sammi Group to make truck and bus axles. Unfortunately, the Sammi venture did not prove successful in the long run, and the joint venture company was ultimately dissolved.

In Japan, Eaton partnered with Nittan Valve to manufacture engine valves. Together, Nittan and Eaton opened a plant in Westminster, South Carolina, that would build parts for Honda and Toyota.[65] According to Larry Oman, retired senior vice president and group executive of Automotive Components:

> *We focused on learning all we could about the Japanese techniques and how they did things, which helped a lot and also helped the company and the division in the long term because we were getting the foreign manufacturers here in the U.S. as customers early on.*[66]

Japanese companies had been using Eaton Roadranger transmissions for years in certain export models. In 1987, through a partnership with Nissan Diesel Motor Company, Eaton developed a U.S.-manufactured transmission specially designed for heavy trucks sold in the Japanese market.[67]

While Eaton did suffer domestically, sales continued to rise in Europe and the Pacific Rim for the company's passenger car and truck components.

Eaton purchased five companies in 1989: King-Seeley (electromechanical and electronic control devices for electric ranges), Tonville (controls and timers for the appliance and automotive industries), AWE Alfons Weiss GmbH (electromechanical and electronic time switches and accessories), Microflex (microelectronic diagnostic technology), and Industrial Data Technologies (industrial workstations).[68]

In 1990, Eaton announced a joint venture with Sumitomo Electric Industries Ltd., a Japanese man-

At the annual shareholders meeting in 1986, E. Mandell "Del" de Windt (right) handed the leadership gavel to James Stover, Eaton's new chairman.

# SANDY CUTLER

ATON CHAIRMAN AND CEO Alexander "Sandy" Cutler has always been a man of action. "You've got two choices," he once told the *New York Times*, noting that he values managers' ability to process information quickly and then act on it. "You can get on with it, or you can stew about it. And you might as well get on with it."[1]

A graduate of Yale University, he studied history and economics with an emphasis on Asian studies, and received an MBA from Dartmouth College. Cutler started out his career as a financial analyst at Cutler-Hammer, the company his great-grandfather founded. By the time Eaton acquired the company in 1978, he had worked his way up to division controller.

At Eaton, Cutler's first assignment was as manager of an electrical equipment factory in Atlanta.[2] There began his steady climb to the top of Eaton's chain of command. In 1986, he became general manager of industrial control and power distribution operations and then president of the industrial group. In 1989, he was promoted to president of the Controls Group, and by 1991, he was elected executive vice president. He rose to chief operating officer in 1995, and in 2000, he was elected chairman and CEO.[3]

John Miller, a longtime member of Eaton's board of directors, recalled that the board noted Cutler's leadership potential early on:

*It is rare to find an individual who has had experience in all areas of the company—some finance, some marketing, some operations. ... We all knew Sandy was a very capable individual. The only question in my mind about Sandy was not whether he was going to be good, but just how good he was going to be.*[4]

When Cutler became CEO, he led the company as it broadened its scope, both externally and internally. According to Victor A. Pelson, a retired Eaton director and former chairman of the AT&T Global Operations Team, "It became clear to Sandy that he needed some outside perspectives and some new vitality in the company. The board and Sandy had discussions about that. He wanted to increase the diversity of the entire organization, including the management team, and that worked out very well."[5]

In addition to valuing swift yet thoughtful action, Cutler places tremendous importance on ethical business values. According to Miller, "He will stress that continuously, 'Yes, we are going to demand performance. We're going to become the premier diversified industrial corporation, the best company in all our markets, but we're going to do it right.'"[6]

Eaton's 1984 hydraulic valve lifter for automobile engines improved gas mileage by 3 percent to 5 percent.

ufacturing and metallurgy technology company, to produce automotive and industrial sintered metal components under the name Engineered Sintered Components Inc.[69]

By 1991, the dollar had fallen, helping make Eaton's export businesses more profitable. The company expected to spend more than a billion dollars in capital investments over the next five years.

## Electric Innovation

In 1976, Congress passed the Electric and Hybrid Vehicle Research, Development, and Demonstration Act. In 1980, Eaton entered into an $8 million, 4-year contract with the U.S. Department of Energy (DOE) to "develop electric propulsion technology for urban delivery-type commercial vehicles."

A 1980 article in the *Cleveland Plain Dealer* reported that Eaton was developing a prototype propulsion system for an electric vehicle program at Cleveland's NASA Lewis Research Center. According to the article, "Eaton became involved in power systems for electric cars in 1976, when it conducted studies of alternate sources of power."[70]

The research team included Eaton's Southfield research center, Eaton's Electric Drives Division, Eagle-Picher Industries, and ASC Inc.[71] Eaton's work on electric vehicles (along with a Detroit Edison project) made news again in 1981, when the DOE faced a possible 50 percent budget cut. However, that did not stop Eaton's research efforts.

Eaton continued working on an alternating current power transmission system that could eventually make the costly direct current systems available at the time obsolete. At the time, General Motors was the only U.S. carmaker with plans to produce electric vehicles.[72] By 1982, Eaton had developed a transaxle for an electric-powered alternating current vehicle, with NASA road testing the prototypes.[73]

According to *Automotive News*, the prototype vehicle, which was finally unveiled in 1989, "meets or exceeds all targeted objectives for efficiency, acceleration, top speed, grade climbing, and braking. The dual shaft electric propulsion (DSEP) team believes it has turned an important page in electric vehicle history by developing a viable transportation alternative based on a systems approach."[74]

Eaton's pioneering work on electrically powered engines would continue to benefit the company for decades to come. Once again, thanks to its substantial, ongoing investment in research and development, Eaton remained on the cutting edge of engineering technology.

Throughout the 1990s, Eaton focused on modernization, streamlining the company's operations while maintaining a global focus that would transform the company into a worldwide powerhouse.

## CHAPTER NINE

# CONTINUED MODERNIZATION

## *1992 – 2000*

*We now manage our enterprise as one integrated operating company. ...*
*It's the Power of One Eaton.*

—2000 Annual Report[1]

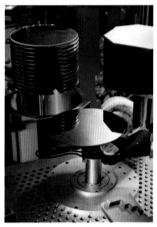

I N 1992, A TEAM OF SENIOR EXECUTIVES reevaluated Eaton's mission. They began by focusing on a statement that founder J. O. Eaton made 80 years earlier: "I can think of no better formula for success than that of producing the highest quality products at costs that make them economically practical in the most competitively priced markets."

The team further elaborated on Eaton Corp.'s future as the company strived to fulfill J. O. Eaton's objectives by adding a new statement to the original:

*To be achieved by our global commitment to:*

- *Customer satisfaction*
- *Profitable growth*
- *Total quality leadership*
- *Continuous productivity improvement*
- *The Eaton Philosophy of excellence through people*
- *Concern for our communities and environment*
- *The highest standard of integrity*[2]

Eaton began the process of reshaping itself from a multinational manufacturing company

into a truly forward-thinking global powerhouse for the 21st century. It was an effort that would take almost a decade and require the vision and dedication of two CEOs and a long-term willingness to ride out fluctuations in the market.

By 1992, Eaton had 38,000 employees organized in seven distinct operations: truck components, engine components, automotive and appliance controls, commercial and military controls, industrial controls and power distribution, hydraulics and general products, and semiconductor equipment.[3]

By 2000, it would become a much larger and more streamlined organization, with four global business units and 63,000 employees. As conceived in 1998 and implemented in 2000, its international scope would broaden from primarily Europe to China, Southeast Asia, and Latin America.[4] Rather than operating business units semi-autonomously as it had in the past, its workforce would follow the same business prac-

Eaton's robotic wafer-handling system set the standard in the semiconductor industry.

tices and code of conduct the world over. It would divest itself of solid businesses that nonetheless lacked a high potential for long-term growth, and acquire companies that, due to advanced technology and a ready customer base, represented industries where Eaton was already a leader.

The company's research and engineering investments would go increasingly toward making "smart" mechanical products—and into developing full assemblies instead of focusing on components manufacturing.[5]

"We said in [Eaton's] early days—and it is still true today—Eaton was very much focused on changing the makeup of the company," explained Craig Arnold, future vice chairman and chief operating officer of Eaton's Industrial sector. "What was historically an automotive and truck company was going to evolve into a diversified industrial company, with the electrical and fluid power business being the two biggest legs on the stool."[6]

### Bringing in Westinghouse

In 1992, Eaton instituted "total quality management across the corporation as a means of improving productivity, building our businesses, and increasing customer satisfaction," according to the company's Annual Report that year. This was the beginning of a shift toward consistency in worldwide operations that by 1998 would evolve into the common set of business practices known as the Eaton Business System.[7]

Along with investing $170 million in research and development, Eaton made three acquisitions in 1992: Franz Kirsten KG, an automotive controls company that doubled Eaton's offerings in that area; Heinemann Electric Company, maker of hydraulic-magnetic circuit breakers; and Illinois Tool Works' automotive switch business, which produced push-button switches for map lights and switches for fog lights and fans.

The March 1994 issue of *Eaton Today* announced Eaton's acquisition of the Westinghouse Distribution and Control Business Unit (DCBU), which prompted an Eaton customer service team in Pennsylvania to uncork a bottle of nonalcoholic champagne.

It was a good time to be in the automobile and truck business. Heavy-duty truck production rose, and light trucks, vans, and SUVs increased in popularity.[8] Still, growth in the electrical controls side of the business remained the top priority as part of an effort to make the company less dependent on the highs and lows of the automobile and truck markets.[9]

"In order to gain greater balance in our earnings and make Eaton less susceptible to cyclical dips in the auto and truck markets, we have committed considerable resources over the past decade to elevate our various controls businesses to leadership levels," stated 1993's letter to shareholders.[10]

Eaton entered the electrical business in the late 1970s with the acquisition of Cutler-Hammer,

This photo from Eaton's 1994 Annual Report depicts the company's Senior Management Council. From left: CEO William Butler; Chief Financial Officer Stephen Hardis; Gerald L. Gherlein; John S. Rodewig; and future CEO Alexander "Sandy" Cutler, then executive vice president and chief operating officer.

and became a leader in the industry in 1994, when it acquired Westinghouse Electric Corp.'s Distribution and Control Business Unit (DCBU) for $1.1 billion. The move, made under the leadership of CEO Bill Butler, who served from 1992 to 1995, tripled Eaton's presence in the industrial controls and power distribution industry.[11]

According to Eli Lustgarten, a Wall Street analyst with Longbow Securities who has been following Eaton for 30 years, the Westinghouse acquisition put Eaton "in the forefront of electrical buyers domestically. It gave [Eaton] critical mass, which they added onto over the years."[12]

The big challenge ahead was to integrate Westinghouse business and Eaton business into a powerful new electrical franchise.[13] According to Stephen Hardis, Eaton's chief financial officer at the time, Eaton approached Westinghouse several times before the 108-year-old company finally agreed to the acquisition. The long-established diversified manufacturing firm had successfully remade itself as a defense contractor in the 1980s but was in financial trouble after diversifying too broadly—venturing into luxury watches, mail-order books and records, real estate development and advertising, and television distribution.

Much of that diversification was financed with assets from Westinghouse Credit Corp., a unit in its Financial Services Division that grew fivefold in the 1980s.[14] However, when the real estate market tanked in the early 1990s, many of Westinghouse

Credit Corp.'s loan customers defaulted. By 1993, Westinghouse was crippled with $5 billion in debt.[15]

"They got themselves into a real financial crisis," recalled Hardis. "The management was forced out, and ... they had to divest some of their businesses, including the Distribution and Control Business Unit (DCBU). It was put up for auction, and we won the auction after, I would say, about a year's negotiation. ... In effect, they dismembered Westinghouse."

Eaton actually wasn't the highest bidder on DCBU. According to Hardis, another company submitted a bid that was $100 million higher than Eaton's. "They took our bid because they felt that once they shook hands [with us] on the deal, they knew what they were going to get," he explained.[16]

Eaton's strong cash flow was "the single most important factor in our ability to build market leadership and to finance the Westinghouse acquisition," stated the 1993 Annual Report.

Eaton had made $1.7 billion in capital improvements since 1984 and invested $2.3 billion in

# EATON BUSINESS SYSTEM

As Eaton continued to set higher goals for faster and more consistent growth, the company sought to create a set of common practices that would allow the company to accelerate growth and improve performance while integrating new acquisitions quickly into the Eaton culture. This led to the creation of the Eaton Business System (EBS).

Under EBS, Eaton was able to build upon the strengths of the lean manufacturing and quality control programs first implemented across the company's separate divisions, such as the Engine Components Operating System first utilized by the Automotive Group.[1] Before

EBS, "Eaton had been a very decentralized company," explained Susan J. Cook, then serving as executive vice president and chief human resources officer at Eaton. "EBS served notice to people, in a kind of a gracious way, that the train is leaving the station, and you're either on it or you're not."[2]

Providing Eaton employees with a shared set of values, philosophies, management tools, and measures, adherence to EBS principles has improved working capital and operating margins while reducing costs and accelerating growth. The six-part system covers corporate goals, achieved in a manner consistent with the Eaton

Philosophy, code of ethics, and Eaton values, as well as strategic, organizational, and profit planning; measuring progress; strategies for growth; recognizing excellence; and sharing established business tools such as Six Sigma to achieve operational excellence.[3]

Led by Eaton CEO Sandy Cutler, EBS was established in 1998. The company newsletter *Eaton Today* described it as "a common management system" for the company that "integrates current strengths, adds new disciplines, sets priorities to direct employee efforts, and aligns the processes we use to guide planning, measure execution, and assess our efforts."[4]

research and development and engineering. It had remained in the top quarter of equity returns among U.S. manufacturing companies in the previous decade, with returns at 16.2 percent. Plans called for Eaton to pay off the debt from the Westinghouse acquisition within five years."[17]

According to a 1993 *New York Times* article on the acquisition, "The deal is an indication that [Westinghouse] is moving steadily ahead with its plan to pay down more than $5 billion in debt left from its disastrous forays into real estate, junk bonds, and loans for leveraged buyouts."[18]

## An Electrical Legacy

Westinghouse had a very long history, surviving the Panic of 1907, the Great Depression, two World Wars, and nearly a dozen recessions. George Westinghouse, who invented the air brake

at age 22, founded Westinghouse in Pittsburgh in 1886.

The company developed the nation's first alternating current (AC) power system in 1891, becoming the primary rival to Thomas Edison's General Electric. In 1893, Westinghouse provided the generator system for the Chicago World's Fair and for the Niagara Falls hydroelectric power station. It was an innovator in the wireless radio field, acquiring numerous patents in that area throughout the 1910s.[19]

In 1919, Westinghouse began manufacturing radio receivers and even set up a radio station in Pittsburgh to provide continuous service to help receiver sales. In the 1930s, the company began mass-producing electric refrigerators, washing machines, and elevators. Westinghouse was a leading government contractor for radar systems during World War II, and after the war developed innova-

According to Cutler:

*EBS will create a culture that will be consistent across the company. We can't continue to do things individually, or 37 ways across all our businesses. ... We need a uniform scorecard, one that can be taken from one business and dropped into another.*[5]

Each division was tasked with determining "what it takes to be a global leader in its market" and coming up with a plan to grow while cutting excess costs and taking into account cultural change.[6] Wall Street analyst Eli Lustgarten considered it the perfect time to revitalize Eaton's corporate culture. As he explained, when Cutler became chairman, "there was a complete cultural change going on—away from a mentality as an automotive and truck supplier, and toward a diversified equipment supplier."[7]

Eaton's evolution proved especially crucial because Eaton was growing at a much faster rate than it had in the past. "Eaton was a relatively slow-growing company for much of its history—and in modern history, was probably growing 3 percent a year," Cook recalled.

At that rate, company culture has time to "percolate," according to Cook. However, since the late 1990s, "we've been in this period of hyper-growth, and it was really important to change how the company was organized."

Traditionally, Eaton had been run almost like a holding company, Cook explained. With EBS, Cutler decided to run Eaton as an integrated operating company, one that united power management under the slogan "The Power of One Eaton."[8] Yannis Tsavalas, Eaton president of Europe, Middle East, and Asia, called EBS "a

very structured approach that helps people understand the interplay among a number of different areas, and how important that interplay is."[9]

According to Gary L. Tooker, a member of Eaton's board of directors since 1992, "Sandy has done an excellent job of getting the entire company on board."[10]

EBS training begins when a manager is hired, and remains ongoing through e-courses and instructor-led classes at Eaton University, the company's management training institute.

The strategy has truly paid off. As Cook added, " 'The Power of One Eaton' is about getting people to think about sharing best practices, sharing points of leverage, having a common supply chain, having one integrated IT system around the world. We think that's been worth three points of margin to us."[11]

tions in nuclear power. By the 1980s, Westinghouse had become a major defense contractor. Its electronic systems business accounted for one-fifth of its sales. By 1990, Westinghouse had shifted its focus from consumer goods to fighter plane radar systems and turbines for power generators.[20]

The deal with Eaton was reached in 1993 and finalized in 1994. The acquisition dramatically altered Eaton's profile. Hardis called it a "transformational" time. Along with the acquisition of Aeroquip-Vickers several years later, according to Hardis, "it made our electrical business and our hydraulic business very large, and once they were integrated, they became very profitable."[21]

Arnaldo Comisso, a retired Eaton vice president who was the manager of a Westinghouse plant in Venezuela and became an Eaton general manager in Brazil after the acquisition, recalled the Westinghouse transition being "extremely smooth."

This was despite the fact that as part of the integration of the Westinghouse acquisition and its existing electrical business, Eaton closed 23 manufacturing, warehousing, and distribution facilities in an effort to cut down on plant capacity and unnecessarily duplicated production capabilities.[22]

"One of the things that was called to my attention at that time was that everybody in the [Westinghouse] organization was very much worried about the transition because they did not know Eaton," Comisso said. "Eaton was not a very well-known name at that time. ... But Eaton respected the value of the people, and in fact, within two or three years, [people] were very happy that they were acquired by Eaton."

Eaton also put tremendous capital into improving Westinghouse's manufacturing facilities. According to Comisso, "They did everything—modernize equipment, new philosophy, business systems. I would say that it was a revolution. Lots of investment ... tremendous modernization—not only equipment, but also in training for people, preparing people for really facing challenges."[23]

Jerry Whitaker, future Eaton president of Electrical for the Americas region, spent 22 years at Westinghouse before he came to Eaton after the acquisition. He recalled:

> First of all, I think the cultures were fairly similar. So I thought the transition was pretty seamless. I mean, the whole integration was well spelled out and well managed, and it was a good combination of both Westinghouse people and Eaton/Cutler-Hammer people.
>
> At the end of the day, I think most of us that came over from Westinghouse feel that it was a better move for all of us and that Eaton has certainly put in the energy, the time, the money, and the focus to grow the electrical business. I'm not sure that Westinghouse would have done that, especially the DCBU end of the business.[24]

## From Multinational to Global

Although Eaton's overseas operations were well established by the early 1990s, according to Hardis, "it was very clear we badly lagged in terms of making Eaton a global company. The increased emphasis on its overseas operations during the 1970s and 1980s has largely been reactionary—a response to increased competition in the United States from foreign manufacturers in Europe and Japan."[25]

Hardis told Cleveland's *Inside Business* magazine that multinational companies of the past had "set up a self-sufficient enterprise in each country in which they wanted to do business, believing that such a local presence would guarantee market share."

This often resulted in overly high costs, redundancies, and inefficient operations. By the 1990s, many trade barriers had begun to dissolve as an increasingly interconnected global market offered substantial opportunities. The trade barriers in those countries ensured corporations operating there would have a price advantage over outsiders.[26] As tariffs began to ease and new customer

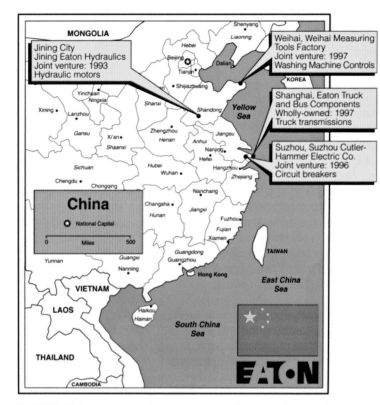

By 1997, Eaton had three joint ventures and one wholly owned subsidiary in China.

bases grew in developing countries across Asia and Latin America, the global marketplace seemed awash in new opportunities.[27]

The challenge was no longer simply to set up shop in a country, but to offer well-designed, economical products that were tailored to customers' needs.[28] According to Hardis:

> We now have to go into these developing countries with world-class operations. We can't go in with a limited investment, send over some old equipment, stick it into a local company, produce an inferior product at a high cost and say, "That's good enough, because there will be a duty that will restrict other people from coming in."
>
> Our competition is going to be coming in from the lowest-cost, most effective sites in the world. Eaton will be a truly global company when whoever runs the business in a particular region is so responsive to customer needs that they are essentially indifferent to where the product is

*made. They just want to make sure the customer gets the best value.*[29]

In 1994, Eaton assembled a task force—composed of young middle-management executives, analysts from the in-house economics department, and overseas managers—to develop a global action plan that set priorities in terms of product lines and countries.[30]

"China was the biggest opportunity," explained Hardis. "India was the second. When you looked at Eaton's products, electrical components, truck transmissions, and hydraulics were the obvious choices. So we made a very conscious decision to invest in those areas."[31]

Eaton had made inroads into China the previous year, when it set up a joint venture with the Jining Hydraulics Components Works of Shandong Province to manufacture low-speed, high-torque hydraulic motors, mainly for farming and construction equipment.[32] A year later, Eaton expanded its electrical business in China with the formation of Cutler-Hammer (Suzhou) Electric Co. Ltd., a joint venture with the Suzhou Electrical Apparatus Group Company (SEAG) to manufacture and sell electrical circuit protection devices. The partnership combined SEAG's strength in the markets it served with one of Cutler-Hammer's strongest product lines.

"We see this agreement as a real benefit to both parties," said CEO Sandy Cutler. "This new partnership allows Eaton to leverage both of these strengths. The spirit of cooperation and understanding that exists between Eaton and SEAG provides a strong foundation for this joint venture."[33]

Eaton's first wholly owned venture in China was established in 1997. The Eaton Truck and Bus Components (Shanghai) Co. Ltd. was a heavy-duty transmission company in the Wai Gao Qiao Free Trade Zone in Pudong District, Shanghai.[34]

In 1998, Eaton launched Eaton Fluid Power (Shanghai) Co. Ltd., a wholly owned hydraulic system company in China. Its product lines included directional control valves, vane pumps, manifold blocks, power systems, hoses, and fittings. Also that year, Eaton joined Nittan Valve in a joint venture called Shanghai Eaton Engine Components Co. Ltd. The company produced engine valves and hydraulic lifters.[35]

## More International Expansion

In 1995, Eaton reported record sales and profits once again. Since 1991, sales had nearly doubled, and net income more than quintupled. That year, Eaton acquired Emwest Products, an Australian switchgear and controls business; IKU Group, a Dutch automotive controls company; and Rubberon Technology Corporation, a golf grip manufacturer based in Thailand.[36]

Eaton's expansion into South Korea was achieved in 1997, when it partnered with a South Korean firm, JC Corporation, in the country's second-largest city, Busan, to manufacture automotive controls. However, when JC Corporation went bankrupt in 1998, Eaton took over the joint venture, renaming it Eaton Automotive Controls, according to C. B. Kim, Eaton's Asia Korea automotive general manager.[37]

In the late 1990s, Eaton's commercial controls included (clockwise from left) power tool switches, Heinemann hydraulic-magnetic circuit breakers, toggle switches for original equipment manufacturers, and rocker switches.

Also in 1997, Eaton opened a plant near Seoul to manufacture limited slip differentials for Hyundai and Kia, both Korean automobile manufacturers.[38] The next year proved challenging as many Asian markets collapsed and Eaton experienced a steep downturn in demand for its semiconductor equipment. However, demand for heavy trucks in North America remained very high.[39]

Latin America was a bright spot on the international horizon. Eaton had maintained a presence there since 1957, when it launched its first South American joint venture with a Brazilian engineering and construction firm. To strengthen its position in an area with expected high growth rates, in 1995, Eaton acquired Mallory Controles of Brazil, which manufactured timers, pressure switches, and water valves.[40]

## Expanding Fluid Power

In 1999, Eaton made its largest acquisition at the time when it purchased Maumee, Ohio–based hydraulics giant Aeroquip-Vickers, a major manufacturer of hoses, couplings, and industrial hydraulics. Aeroquip-Vickers had 15,000 employees, 50 plants in 15 countries, and $2.2 billion in annual sales—double that of the Westinghouse DCBU when Eaton acquired that operation.

Eaton purchased Aeroquip-Vickers in February of that year at a premium price of approximately $1.7 billion, or $58 a share.[41] According to analyst Kent Mortensen of Robert W. Baird & Company Inc., quoted in the *New York Times* after the announcement of the sale, the acquisition would strengthen Eaton's stance against the industrial hydraulics

# ACCELERATED GROWTH

IN 2000, EATON SET IN MOTION A strategy for accelerated growth. For the first time, Eaton publicly announced its revenue, profitability, working capital, and return on capital goals for the next five years—before it even announced those goals internally. The company aimed to grow at a breathtaking 10 percent annually.

"We really wanted to get Eaton balanced on three dimensions," explained CEO Sandy Cutler. "The first dimension was better business balance, and we've really achieved that now with 70 percent of it in aerospace, hydraulics, and electrical. The second was geographic balance. It's great when the U.S. economy is going strong to be able to be U.S.-oriented, but through the

cycle, there are going to be times when that won't be as true."[1]

The third dimension was to improve the balance in Eaton's business cycle. Eaton previously had large investments in the early phase of the standard three-phase economic cycle. "So, early in the economic cycle, the truck business would pick up strongly," Cutler said. "Then residential housing would pick up strongly. That's where Eaton had large investments and did quite well. What we wanted to do was find a balance—a third early, a third mid, and a third late."[2]

To do that, Eaton focused on building up aerospace, a late-cycle business, and hydraulics, a mid-cycle business. According to Cutler,

"Today, we are very well balanced. ... That's one of the marks of a really good diversified industrial—they participate consistently right through the economic cycle."

Wall Street was initially dubious about Eaton's 2000 plan for accelerated growth, but by 2005, the company had hit the mark. "In 2005, we announced the next round, which are goals for 2010, and they are equally as bold," Cutler said.

In Asia, for example, Eaton had under $700 million in annual revenue in 2005. "We said we wanted to be $2.5 billion by 2010," says Cutler. "People looked at that and said, 'Oh my God, how is that going to happen?' We'll get there, and ahead of schedule."[3]

Eaton acquired Aeroquip-Vickers in 1999. At the time, it was Eaton's largest acquisition.

Eaton Today

Volume 14
Issue 2
February 1999

Published Monthly for the Employees of Eaton Corporation

*Largest acquisition in Eaton history*

# Aeroquip-Vickers to join Eaton family

Eaton and Aeroquip-Vickers, Inc., jointly announced on February 1 that Eaton will acquire all of the outstanding common shares of Aeroquip-Vickers for \$58 per share in cash, or approximately \$1.7 billion. The Boards of Directors of both companies have approved the transaction, which is subject to normal government reviews and the approval of Aeroquip-Vickers shareholders. Completion is expected in April.

Chairman Stephen R. Hardis said, "We are very pleased to welcome Aeroquip-Vickers to the family of Eaton businesses. Leadership is a fundamental requisite for success in today's global economy. This acquisition enables Eaton to achieve that critical objective—building upon and extending Eaton's strong position in mobile hydraulics. With Vickers, we acquire a global leader in industrial hydraulics and the combined scale of \$1.1 billion to serve mobile and industrial customers. This complementary acquisition fundamentally repositions our business among the world leaders, just as our 1993 acquisition of the Westinghouse DCBU did for our Cutler-Hammer business.

"With Aeroquip, we expand upon these strengths in hydraulics via its \$1.1 billion position in hose and

*The Vickers main engine-driven pump supplies pressure for an aircraft's primary hydraulic system. The Aeroquip hose assembly conveys the hydraulic pressure through the system.*

couplings, serving mobile and industrial, aerospace and automotive customers. Together, Eaton and Aeroquip-Vickers create an aerospace hydraulics business with sales of \$700 million, and a systems capability across all hydraulics applications that is unparalleled.

**The following message was e-mailed to employees on February 1, 1999.**

Today's announcement of the proposed acquisition of Aeroquip-Vickers represents a very exciting strategic opportunity for the corporation. During 1997, we gained great momentum in the execution of our Growth Strategy. We blew through our 1997 profit plan earnings commitment and made a number of major acquisition and divestiture moves which enhanced our long-term growth potential. In 1998, however, as a result of a number of factors, we lost that momentum. The effects are painfully apparent in our stock price and our sense of internal confidence.

Now we have a great chance to regain the rhythm of our execution of our reaching, long-term plans. This acquisition epitomizes the type of major move we have been targeting in order to strengthen our major businesses. The integration of Aeroquip-Vickers into Eaton will represent a major effort, and we know from the DCBU acquisition that the effects will be borne by a great number of our people. But, the benefits will be significant for all Eaton employees. In order to capitalize on this opportunity, we will only need to execute our integration plan, but we have to at least meet our 1999 Profit Plan commitments. It is also critical that we execute our new product growth programs successfully. Our financing plans for the acquisition have been designed consciously so that we can continue to finance our growth plans in each of our existing businesses. By accomplishing these objectives, we will be back on track with our goal of creating an enterprise capable of 10 percent sustainable earnings growth.

As more information becomes available regarding this exciting acquisition, we will be communicating the important details.

We know we can count on your support.

*Steve Hardis*
Chairman and Chief Executive Officer

*Sandy Cutler*
President and Chief Operating Officer

**A special report on the acquisition will appear in next month's Eaton Today.**

"The value created for our customers and our owners from this combination will be significant, with mature-year synergies of about \$120 million. We expect the acquisition to be neutral to Eaton earnings this year, excluding first-year transition (continued on page 2)

**H I G H L I G H T S**

**Aeroquip-Vickers Headquarters** in Maumee, Ohio, sits on 49 acres. The facility was built in 1989.

*Story on page 2*

**Engine valves aren't the only things** manufactured at this plant in São Jose dos Campos, Brazil. Minan Aparecida Soares packages valves for shipping.

*Story on page 3*

**Almost as much a part of London as Big Ben.** The London taxi is a fixture in England and Eaton's Commercial Controls Division supplies components for these icons.

*Story on page 3*

**Arch-ya' glad Cutler-Hammer came to this monument's rescue?!** The Gateway Arch in St. Louis, Missouri, had its main switchboard replaced by Cutler-Hammer.

*Story on page 4*

---

leader, Cleveland-based Parker Hannifin Corp. "They are still No. 2, but they're a much more formidable competitor with a broader product line," Mortensen said of Eaton.[42]

Aeroquip's history dated back to 1939, when a young engineer named Peter F. Hurst relocated to the United States as a manager of the U.S. operations for a Berlin-based aircraft brake company. In his new role, he led a team that came up with a revolutionary design for detachable hose fittings for aircraft brake mechanisms. The new design replaced inefficient permanently attached hoses that, when worn out, required the replacement of an aircraft's entire brake mechanism.

Hurst then licensed the patents, and with the help of several investors, began manufacturing the hydraulic devices in a reconditioned milk processing plant. The company grew quickly, although after the start of World War II, Hurst had to step down because he was a German citizen. Nearly two years later, however, he was able to rejoin the company, and in 1945 he became an American citizen.[43]

In the 1950s and 1960s, Aeroquip made a number of significant acquisitions, including Marman Products Company, a manufacturer of clamp couplings and straps for airplanes that was founded by Herbert "Zeppo" Marx of the Marx Brothers. It launched operations in Mexico and Brazil in 1965.

In 1968, Aeroquip merged with a Toledo glass company, Libbey-Owens-Ford, which provided the financing it needed to grow internationally. In 1989, Aeroquip underwent reorganization under a new parent company, TRINOVA, combining forces with a plastic molding company.[44]

Los Angeles entrepreneur Harry F. Vickers founded Vickers Inc. in 1921. He moved the company to Detroit eight years later, where it became a diversified maker of hydraulic pumps, transmissions, valves, and controls. The company was sold to Sperry in 1937, and then became part of the newly merged Sperry Rand Corporation in

1955. Libbey-Owens-Ford bought Vickers from Sperry in the early 1980s.[45]

Prior to the Aeroquip-Vickers acquisition, Eaton had only been a minor player in the fluid power industry. According to an article in the *Cleveland Plain Dealer*:

*[The acquisition] allowed Eaton to create a much bigger and stronger hydraulics business, especially in farm and construction equipment. It also strengthened the company's aerospace controls business and gave Eaton an entry into the tubes, hoses, and fittings markets.*

*Eaton not only gained new markets, but also broadened its product lines so that it could offer customers entire systems, not just parts. It also*

This stylized rendition from the 1999 Annual Report illustrates Eaton and Vickers aerospace components. These products and systems were engineered to solve specific customer needs in aerospace and allied fields and generated more than $700 million in sales.

*gained opportunities to make 'smart components' by applying new electronic technologies to mechanical parts.*[46]

Jeff Finch, former Aeroquip marketing director and vice president and general manager of the Eaton Hydraulics Group's fluid conveyance products, said that due to Eaton's financial strength and understanding of the hydraulics business, Aeroquip-Vickers employees "quickly came to the understanding that Eaton was very serious and

desirous of being in this whole fluid power space, both hydraulic components and hose products. Eaton had much more wherewithal to expand our presence in the industry than probably Aeroquip-Vickers was ever going to have on its own."[47]

According to the *Plain Dealer*, at the start, "some analysts questioned whether Eaton had overpaid and incurred too much debt."[48] However, by June 2000, analysts such as Andrew Casey of Midwest Research in Cleveland had come to consider the acquisition a sage move. Noting that Eaton "enters into only those acquisitions that have a significant strategic fit and have a strong potential to add to earnings in the near future," Casey said the Aeroquip-Vickers acquisition made Eaton "a very formidable competitor in the fluid power segment."[49]

Once the acquisition was complete, Eaton embarked on the challenge of creating "one business and one culture out of what was arguably, at least three," explained Craig Arnold, vice chairman and chief operating officer of the Industrial Sector. "That was certainly one of the big challenges in the early days—picking a management team and getting [them] to develop a shared sense of purpose, rationalizing our approach to the market, developing the appropriate manufacturing footprint around our resources, and putting them in places that made sense to serve our customers globally."[50]

Part of Eaton's strategy with Aeroquip-Vickers included assembling a full-time integration task force composed of about 20 employees.[51] "There were a lot of very good processes inside of Aeroquip," Arnold said. "A lot of the processes that were embedded in that business actually became Eaton processes."[52]

Arnold believed that Eaton's most important contribution, however, was its "financial wherewithal to reinvest in the business. [Aeroquip-Vickers] was a business that had not been invested in at the rate that it should have been over the last few years. So we really brought a new focus on organic growth, product development, and innovation."[53]

Bill Blausey, Eaton senior vice president and chief information officer, said that the Vickers side of the business was brought into the fold more quickly than Aeroquip because Vickers "had more

Right: By 1997, Eaton led the automotive industry in highly engineered fan drives and fans to cool engines.

Below: Craig Arnold, future vice chairman and chief operating officer of Eaton's Industrial Sector, served as senior vice president and group executive for the company's fluid power segment in 2000.

operational issues in the plants, and so Eaton focused there, rightly so, in bringing them under the Eaton umbrella."[54]

According to Blausey, "Interestingly enough, the products were certainly more the kinds of products that Eaton wanted on the Vickers side, but the processes and the way we operated were more effective on the Aeroquip side and probably became as valuable to Eaton over time as the companies were integrated."[55]

### New Energy for a New Millennium

By 1999, Eaton had 63,000 employees and 195 manufacturing sites across 23 countries. That year, the company divested itself of three businesses: a viscous fan drive business, Engineered Fasteners, and Vickers Electronic Systems' computer numerical controls business.

Eaton also expanded its Athens, Georgia, plant to meet all of Mercedes-Benz's supercharger requirements and built a heavy-duty truck transmission plant in San Luis Potosí, Mexico, and a hydraulics hose and fittings plant in Querétaro, Mexico. In addition, the company won a Federal Aviation Administration contract to develop arc fault technology to reduce fire hazards on board aircraft.[56]

By the turn of the new century, Eaton had refocused into four global business units: Fluid Power, Electrical, Automotive, and Truck, united by the Eaton Business System. "We now manage our enterprise as one integrated operating company, not four individual businesses," stated the 2000 Annual Report. "It's the Power of One Eaton: Harnessing Eaton's size, strength, and scope through the common tools and processes of the Eaton Business System to drive change and rapidly leverage best practices across the organization."[57]

Fluid Power and Industrial and Commercial Controls were Eaton's largest business segments, bringing in 62 percent of the company's operating profit. The company further expanded its reach by acquiring three more fluid power businesses in different parts of the world. Eaton also announced an intent to purchase Sumitomo's 50 percent interest in Sumitomo Eaton Hydraulics Co. As the company strengthened its focus on its most profitable segments, it sold its Vehicle Switch/Electronics Division and its power tool switch

Above: The electronic modules shown in this 1994 photo were part of Eaton's new multiplexing system for Chrysler's 1996 Jeep Grand Cherokee, which featured remote keyless entry, single/all-door lock, auto door lock at 15 mph, heated mirrors, and driver's side window express-down. The assembler in the photo is Veronica Rosas Perez of Eaton's Matamoros, Mexico, plant.

Right: By the late 1990s, Eaton had become one of the world's top suppliers of semiconductor manufacturing equipment.

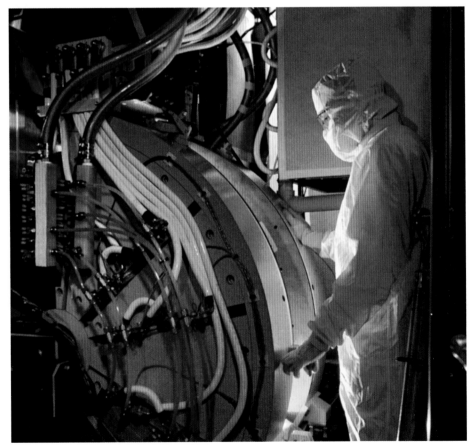

product line. It also spun off its semiconductor equipment business, creating more than $1 billion in shareholder value.[58]

Eaton's three-part strategy to investigate the company's growth rates and increase profitability included diversifying the mix of its businesses to increase its geographic footprint and restore balance throughout the economic cycle, while at the same time using the Eaton Business System to run the company more effectively. Eaton also focused on upgrading its leadership talents. According to the 2000 Annual Report, by the start of the new millennium, approximately 47 percent of senior managers had held their jobs for a year or less, the result of new talent brought in from the outside as well as many internal promotions, moves designed to stabilize Eaton's leadership team. Hybrid technology and environmentally friendly emissions sys-

tems were identified as promising growth markets, and Eaton continued developing air management systems that increased fuel economy and improved emissions control.

The company publicly announced its revenue, profitability, working capital, and ROIC goals for the next five years for the first time and also began the practice of providing quarterly guidance to investors. Eaton announced a goal of 10 percent revenue growth each year for the next five years, and placed increased emphasis on cross-company collaboration focused on research and product development. As Eaton continued to prosper and solidify its position as a market leader, *IndustryWeek* magazine named Eaton one of the world's top 100 best-managed companies, making special note of the Eaton Business System.[59]

As the world's demand for energy continues to grow, Eaton has proven itself a global leader in providing reliable, efficient, and safe power management solutions for an increasing number of industries. *(Photo © iStockphoto.com/David Elfstrom.)*

## CHAPTER TEN

# A GREEN (SUSTAINABLE) FUTURE

## 2000 AND BEYOND

*To say that 2001 was a difficult year is to vastly understate the challenges faced by our corporation and the community we call the civilized world. Our end markets weakened, the economy declined, and the world changed.*

—Chairman and CEO Sandy Cutler[1]

T HERE WAS A CONSIDERABLE DECLINE in the global economy throughout the early part of the decade, as stocks tumbled after the collapse of the technology boom of the 1990s. This was accompanied by a recession that affected the European Union throughout 2000 and 2001. Global conditions were exacerbated by the horrific September 11, 2001, terrorist attacks, which had long-ranging detrimental effects on the U.S. economy. Eaton executives soon began to feel the first effects of the sharp downturn in the North American industrial economies.

Despite the difficult economic climate, Eaton publicly announced its first set of financial goals for the company in 2000, setting the pace for an aggressive period of growth. The company set ambitious goals as part of its successful five year strategy, promising to grow revenues by 10 percent per year, improve profitability by 30 percent, and reduce capital intensity by 25 percent.[2]

While Eaton would eventually reach its stated goals, by mid-2001 quarterly revenues were dropping. Second quarter 2001 revenues were $1.87 billion, as compared with $2.17 billion in the second quarter of 2000, a 14 percent drop. "There's no question these are difficult times for U.S. manufacturing and even for diversified indus-

trials like Eaton," Chairman and CEO Sandy Cutler admitted.[3]

### A New Eaton

A transformation was in order, and it began at the very top. From 2000 to 2002, Eaton brought in a slew of new executives, replacing nearly half of its management structure. Eaton's strategy throughout the decade included targeted divestitures of businesses with total annual sales of more than $1.8 billion and acquisitions totaling more than $6 billion in revenues, such as taking its Eaton Semiconductor Equipment subsidiary public in 2000. Eaton later sold its share of the entire business and sold its automotive controls business in 2007.[4]

The company made a concerted effort to increase the international side of the business, raising its proportion of overseas sales from 20 percent at the start of the decade to 55 percent by the end of 2010, with sales in the devel-

Eaton Chairman and CEO Sandy Cutler has successfully led the company through an era of growth and evolution. *(Photo © 2007 Roger Mastroianni.)*

oping world rising from 8 percent to 25 percent in the same time frame. At the same time, Eaton sought to achieve balance throughout fluctuating global economic business cycles.

To achieve these goals, Eaton instituted a number of internal changes, including bringing in a fresh new management talent. According to Stephen Buente, retired senior vice president of the Automotive Group, "We realized we had to really change the culture, and we had to do it quickly, which in a company the size of Eaton is a massive undertaking and tough to make work."[5]

Acquisitions would also prove crucial to Eaton's growth strategy, with newly acquired companies expected to bring in 40 percent of the total sales growth from 2000 to 2005.[6] The entire company attitude changed internally, shifting the priority from yearly incremental improvements to a direct focus on increasing market share and outperforming the competition.[7] As part of the company's rededicated approach to successful acquisitions, Eaton set high performance standards for the businesses it acquired, closely monitoring their growth from year to year.[8] Eaton made many significant acquisitions throughout the decade, including major acquisitions in aerospace and electrical, such as the acquisition of the Moeller and Phoenixtec electrical businesses.

In 2002, Eaton announced its plans to acquire Boston Weatherhead from the Dana Corporation. Employing 1,049 people and bringing in $207 million in sales in 2001, Boston Weatherhead manufactured hose tubing and fluid connections for fluid power systems, primarily for industrial distribution, mobile off-highway, and heavy-duty truck markets.[9] Boston Weatherhead's strong brand name and full line of complementary products supported Eaton's strategy to enhance its capabilities as a provider to the fluid power industry.[10]

Once the acquisition was complete, the process of integrating Boston Weatherhead into Eaton's Fluid Power segment began. To improve efficiency and eliminate redundancy, Eaton decided to close its hose plant in North Carolina and consolidate its production with a similar Boston Weatherhead plant in Tennessee. Boston Weatherhead's Tennessee headquarters was also closed, and its plants in Mississippi and Ohio were moved to a newly purchased Eaton plant in Gainesboro, Tennessee.[11]

From 2002 to 2003, despite the stagnancy in its end markets, Eaton managed to surpass its targets, with total sales growth of more than 12 percent. Sales increased from $7.2 billion in 2002 to $8.1 billion in 2003.[12]

Although the company grew quickly, it did not lose sight of its principles. In 2003, all Eaton employees received a foundational course in Eaton's Code of Ethics as part of the company's continued reinforcement of its corporate values. "While some organizations may regard statements of ethics and values as superfluous, we do not," stated the 2003 Annual Report.[13]

Eaton also strengthened its Global Ethics program by establishing an ombuds program and by publishing its ethics guide in more than 30 languages. Ombuds provided objective, confidential guidance to employees in resolving work-related problems, while the Global Ethics program featured a helpline for Eaton-related ethical issues.[14]

From its firm foundations as a values-based organization, Eaton remained dedicated to providing its employees with the best possible work environment. The company took care not to emphasize the difference between employee ranks, creating a collegial culture where everyone was equal and dedicated to the same goals.[15]

Eaton also instituted an annual survey of all of its employees, allowing every member of Eaton's workforce to provide confidential feedback that helped guide the company's direction. According to Sue Cook, former executive vice president of Human Resources, "The annual employee survey and Eaton's active response to its results are key reasons why we retain talented and engaged employees."[16]

## Success in Aerospace

Throughout the decade, Eaton made a considerable effort to develop its aerospace business. From bringing in under $200 million in sales at the time of the Aeroquip-Vickers acquisition in 1999, Eaton grew its aerospace business through growth and acquisitions to sales of $1.7 billion. Acquisitions in the aerospace business included Cobham's fuel system business, PerkinElmer's aerospace business, and Argo-Tech's fuel system business.

Aerospace won $2 billion in commercial and military contracts in 2001, principally to develop fluid power systems for Lockheed Martin's Joint Strike Fighter.[17] By 2002, Eaton's aerospace business was bringing in approximately $700 million in annual sales. Eaton's aerospace business nearly doubled in 2005 due to two acquisitions. In September 2005, Eaton acquired the fuel system business of Cobham plc, a British company. The fuel system business had sales of $210 million in 2004. Cobham's product lines added to Eaton's offerings in fluid conveyance and pump technology and expanded its European presence in the commercial and defense industries.[18]

A month later, Eaton entered into an agreement to purchase Maryland-based PerkinElmer's aerospace business for $333 million. A leading provider of sealing and pneumatic systems for large commercial aircraft and regional jets, the company had

950 employees and overseas operations in France and Indonesia.[19]

Eaton's international growth in the aerospace business has proven especially prescient. According to Don McGrath, senior vice president of communications, "We continue to see overseas growth, including entering into joint ventures in Russia and China as they're trying to build their aerospace and aviation industries. Both Russia and China want to be able to build [a single aisle] aircraft to compete with Airbus and Boeing. And certainly China, as you know—well, when they put their mind to something, they usually deliver. These are areas where we see significant growth potential."

Eaton's philosophy regarding aerospace acquisitions has been to use excellence in components to also offer subsystems and increasingly complete systems. Brad Morton, president of Eaton's aerospace business, explained:

*We believe the intellectual property and the technology introduction at a component level is what makes systems integration effective. We believe*

In 2001, Eaton won $2 billion in commercial and military aerospace contracts, including a contract to develop the fluid power system for the Lockheed Martin Joint Strike Fighter.

Integrated Hydraulics, based in Warwick, UK, specialized in manufacturing hydraulic integrated circuits. In 2008, Eaton acquired Integrated Hydraulic's parent company, Integ Holdings, a UK-based manufacturer of screw-in cartridge valves, custom-engineered hydraulic valves, and manifold systems (inset). Shown below are workers assembling components at an Integrated Hydraulics plant in Warwick, UK.

*that you've got to have control of that intellectual property and of the technology at a component level in order to be a very good systems integrator and optimizer of systems.*[20]

Eaton's continued focus on acquisition targets that complement its technological offerings on a component level has played a major role in allowing Eaton to better serve its customers with a wide portfolio of products. The acquisitions of Cobham's fuel system business, PerkinElmer's aerospace business, and Argo-Tech helped Eaton expand that portfolio and transform the company into one of the most comprehensive hydraulic, electrical, fuel system, and pneumatic suppliers in the world.[21]

Putting all those components together, Eaton can deliver products such as the complete fuel sys-

tem for Cessna's new Citation Columbus aircraft, a business jet that Eaton has been involved with since 2008, with the first flight scheduled for 2011.[22]

## Electrical Overhaul

Eaton's electrical business stood at a crossroads in 2001. The electrical business' annual sales were less than $2 billion and the great majority of these sales were in the U.S. Sales took a significant hit during the 2001 recession. Eaton launched an ambitious plan to build the business. The company changed the management structure, bringing in executive talent from across the industry who worked closely with existing leadership. Only after cutting costs dramatically could Eaton's electrical business begin to truly focus on growth.

New acquisitions were targeted, particularly outside the United States.

The acquisition of the electrical business segments of UK-based Delta in 2003 included brands such as Mem, Holec, Bill, Home Automation, Elek, and Tabula. Besides the well-recognized brands it acquired, Eaton also gained new distribution channels throughout the globe, improving the company's presence across Western Europe, the Middle East, China, Southeast Asia, and Australia.[23] According to Chairman and CEO Sandy Cutler, the Delta acquisition was expected to "greatly strengthen Eaton's ability to support our multinational customers in our electrical business."[24]

In 2003, Eaton launched a joint venture with Caterpillar Inc. operating under the name Intelligent Switchgear Organization LLC. The new venture produced the paralleling switchgear required for interfacing backup generation within a power grid.

In 2004, Eaton earned a record $9.8 billion in sales. That year, Eaton also acquired Powerware for $560 million, the third-largest acquisition in its history. A global leader in uninterruptible power supply (UPS) systems, DC power products, and power quality services, Powerware had $775 million in revenues in 2003. Based in Raleigh, North Carolina, Powerware had a diverse customer base that included computer manufacturers, industrial companies, government telecommunications firms, hospitals, and data centers.

The Powerware acquisition not only brought new products to Eaton, it gave the company a

stronger international presence. According to Frank Campbell, president of the Europe, Middle East, and Africa region for the Electrical Group:

*We identified the electrical business as a really good place to be, and so we made the strategic decision to not only be a power distribution and control equipment company but to go into this power quality space. So we made a series of acquisitions, again, very strategically, the biggest one of which was Powerware. Powerware was a great acquisition. It was a fabulous acquisition. It gave us a really strong global presence.*[25]

## A Perfect Fit

In October 2007, Eaton further established its presence in Europe, the Middle East, and Africa with its acquisition of the small systems business of Schneider Electric's MGE UPS Systems for $612 million. Based in Saint-Ismier, France, MGE had 800 employees and a presence in more than 40 countries. Its products included uninterruptible power supply systems, power distribution units, static transfer switches, and surge suppressors. The company had a sales volume of $167 million for the 12-month period ending September 30, 2007.

Later in December 2007, Eaton made its largest acquisition announcement to date, signifying its intention to purchase Taiwan-based Phoenixtec and German-based Moeller, a leading European company specializing in industrial controls and power distribution. Altogether, the Phoenixtec and Moeller acquisitions totaled a purchase price of more than $2.8 billion. With combined estimated sales of $2 billion in 2007, both of the new acquisitions significantly strengthened the global presence of Eaton's electrical business.

Based in Bonn, Germany, the Moeller Group supplied components for commercial and residential building applications, as well as industrial controls for industrial equipment applications. Its primary markets were Western and Eastern Europe, but it also had a growing presence in Asia. At the

In 2007, Eaton acquired Taiwan-based Phoenixtec, which specialized in uninterruptible power supply systems.

time of Eaton's $2 billion acquisition of the company, Moeller had 8,700 employees.[26]

Moeller was founded in 1899 as a switchgear production company in Cologne, Germany. After World War II, it began delivering switchgear to electrical wholesalers, expanding to 1,500 employees and generating sales of 30 million deutsche marks. In the 1950s, its product innovations included FAK foot and palm switches, four-pole contactors, compact circuit breakers, and fully insulation-enclosed power distribution systems.

By the 1970s, Moeller's workforce grew to 5,000 employees, and sales expanded to South America, Japan, and Australia. The expansion continued until 2003, when a worldwide economic downturn prompted the sale of the company to a group of U.S. investors. In 2005, the British private equity firm Doughty Hanson & Co. acquired a majority stake in the group.[27]

The Moeller acquisition substantially increased Eaton's European presence in electrical power distribution and control products. Moeller not only allowed Eaton to expand its product offerings, it also gave the company access to a knowledgeable, experienced sales and support staff on the global playing field. According to Frank Campbell, "[Moeller] had really great technology. They had a really great manufacturing footprint. They had really great people. They had a really great commercial presence globally. So with that acquisition, we were able to truly change the game, and actually put Eaton on the international electrical competitive map."[28]

Eaton began working on a plan to provide its customers with complete, comprehensive solutions for their power systems needs. Known as PowerChain Management, the system helped Eaton customers improve their operational efficiency, strengthen safety standards, mitigate risks, and provide increased reliability overall. To ensure it would be able to provide its customers with such wide-ranging solutions, the company focused on acquisitions that would fill in any gaps in Eaton's product and distribution network. "We launched PowerChain as a way to tell our customers that it's far better to buy all the chain links from one manufacturer because you get an integrated strategy for safety, reliability, and backup," explained Thomas Gross, vice chairman and chief financial officer of the electrical sector.[29]

100 years.
History of our time. Spirit of our time. Signs of our time.

MOELLER

Eaton acquired power distribution and industrial controls specialist Moeller in 2007. The company already had a long history that began in 1899 in Cologne, Germany, with the manufacture of switching devices.

Moeller possessed both the products and the distribution channels throughout Europe and Asia that would help Eaton successfully offer its PowerChain Management solutions across the globe. While Eaton had already established a strong power distribution portfolio in North America, the Moeller acquisition helped set Eaton up as a major competitor in the electrical products business outside North America.[30] The fact that Moeller already had a significant, well-known presence in the markets it served was one of the many reasons Eaton was interested in the acquisition in the first place.[31]

Eaton also expanded its global presence when it acquired Phoenixtec. Established in 1978 and based in Taipei, Taiwan, Phoenixtec employed 5,800 people by 2007 and was a public company listed on the Taiwan Stock Exchange. Phoenixtec specialized in manufacturing single- and three-phase uninterruptible power supply systems sold mainly in China and parts of Europe, and its technology leadership and manufacturing facilities were based in China and Taiwan. Eaton acquired Phoenixtec for $568 million.[32]

Along with its customer base, Phoenixtec proved appealing to Eaton due to its low-cost manufacturing capability. With the Phoenixtec acquisition, Eaton became the No. 2 supplier of small UPS systems. "It really helped with the small product strategy, allowing us to compete," said Randy Carson, retired president of Eaton's Electrical Group.[33]

Although Phoenixtec was only about a third of the size of Moeller, it soon proved to be just as important an acquisition. Eaton already had several manufacturing plants in China at the time of the acquisition, but Phoenixtec allowed Eaton to immediately broaden its manufacturing presence in China. In addition, Phoenixtec was the leading supplier of small UPS systems in China.[34]

Both Moeller and Phoenixtec were in the process of integration throughout 2008 and 2009. According to James W. McGill, executive vice president and chief human resources officer as well as former president of the Asia Pacific region, "The people in Phoenixtec are genuinely excited about being part of the Eaton family. They see substantial growth opportunities for themselves."[35]

The Moeller acquisition involved integrating a larger and in some ways more complex company.[36] According to Mark M. McGuire, Eaton's executive vice president and general counsel, "Rather than completely engulfing them in Eaton, we want to make sure that we do it in such a way that we preserve the company's values and also learn from what they have—their own people, systems, and operations, to make sure that we don't miss any opportunities to make the whole of Eaton better by learning from what they're doing."[37]

## A Global Marketplace

By the late 1990s, Eaton had recognized Asia as a region ripe for growth, with developing nations such as China and India building infrastructure at a dizzying pace. In 2005, as Asia became a major focus for Eaton's growth strategy, the company set a goal of $2.5 billion in sales for the region by 2010. Eaton's annual revenues in the region jumped from $100 million to $1.1 billion between 1996 and 2008, representing an astounding 26 percent per year growth rate.[38]

Along with Delta plc and Powerware, Eaton would acquire several other companies that were either based in China or had a substantial business presence in the country, including Winner Group Holdings and Changzhou Senyuan.[39]

By 2008, Eaton had gone from employing hundreds of people in China to more than 10,000. Eaton's deliberate efforts to seek expansion in the region would help the company continue to grow as the world began to struggle with a deep, global recession that shook international markets through the end of the decade. Nicholas Heymann, an industrial analyst, predicted that during the global recession, "China's plan to spend millions of dollars to stave off its own economic downturn should help Eaton, because much of the money will go toward the nation's infrastructure," which included power generation facilities, roads, and vehicles.[40]

At the same time, Eaton recognized that its expanding global reach meant the company had to pay careful attention to the balance between its domestic and international markets. According to Sandy Cutler:

> As the company has grown substantially outside of the United States, I think there has been a very clear recognition that we needed to have management located in the region where we're doing business to ensure that we have fast decision making, rather than all decisions having to come back to headquarters, regardless of whether the headquarters were in the U.S., Europe, or Asia.

By increasing its market presence in developing countries such as China, India, and Brazil, Eaton significantly improved its global balance.[41] Other indicators drove Eaton's prescient decision as well, such as the opportunities in China's vehicle markets. Eaton's advanced hybrid electric systems technology proved an excellent match for the most populous nation in the world. China's increased emphasis on sustainable development while reducing the country's levels of pollution and carbon

# REGIONALIZATION

B Y 2009, ABOUT 55 PERCENT OF Eaton's sales were outside the United States. Although Eaton continued to utilize its effective Eaton Business System to ensure efficient operations, the company recognized that increasing speed while remaining agile and innovative would require it to allow its international business to operate more locally.

Eaton's goal was to build its capabilities in each region, while empowering local management so that they could make rapid business decisions that would allow them to respond to their customers quickly and efficiently.[1]

Eaton's dedicated efforts to adapt to the ever-changing global markets remained a priority even in the face of adversity. According to Chairman and CEO Sandy Cutler:

*In the midst of the recession, when it would have been easy not to have to change the organization, we made the decision that because of the very fast growth we had in our international regions, as well as our large acquisitions, we needed to regionalize not only our business operating decisions but also our functional operating decisions. It's still necessary to coordinate many things on an international basis, but we're really trying to work on the issue of speed and agility within the local markets.[2]*

emissions gave Eaton important opportunities to expand its presence in the country.[42]

As Eaton grew internationally, the company focused on maintaining a highly dedicated workforce. Eaton's efforts to recruit talented employees involves teams of dedicated recruiters located in the company's largest markets, including the United States, Mexico, Brazil, Europe, India, and China. "Those groups are focused on the talented people that we recruit to fill our jobs," explained James McGill, executive vice president and chief human resources officer.[43]

## Helping Out

After Hurricane Katrina hit New Orleans and the Gulf Coast in August 2005, Eaton played an important role in refurbishing and replacing electrical systems, and helping restore power to government agencies, hospitals, and businesses.[44] Along with backup power generating equipment and power distribution products, Eaton sent a team of engineers and other support staff to the area to help affected customers and partners. In the weeks that followed, Eaton also donated power generators to those affected by the hurricane.

When the Louisiana Energy Company's refinery became inoperable after it was flooded with several feet of seawater and mud, Eaton workers were on the scene almost immediately, mobilizing resources and surveying the damage by helicopter. All told, 125 Eaton personnel focused on the refinery's recovery effort, assessing damage, reconditioning circuit breakers, and providing replacement parts. They also provided testing, commissioning, and start-up services of electrical equipment and uninterruptible power supply systems, ensuring that all electrical systems were in proper working order. Impressed by the quick and thorough response, the energy company awarded Eaton a national contract.[45]

Subsequently, Eaton worked with oil drilling companies along the coastline to develop anti-corrosion hydraulic cylinders that would allow offshore drilling platforms to endure strong waves and currents while drilling deeper.[46]

Eaton's culture of community support was also apparent in a very different context in 2008. As Eaton's reach expanded in Asia, so did its philanthropic efforts there. "We felt it was important to demonstrate to the local community that we were committed because the company [we acquired] had been known for its community involvement," explained Barry Doggett, Eaton's senior vice president of public and community affairs.[47]

In 2008, when Eaton acquired Changzhou Senyuan Switch Co. Ltd. an electrical manufacturing firm about three hours from Shanghai, it made a donation to the local school. According to Doggett:

*The employees were very pleased by this, but said, "Well, we've got an interest of our own—a local orphanage. We would like, at the same time you're announcing this, to be able to get involved with that."*

*So there ended up being two major activities that took place, one totally employee-driven, and the other driven by a broader interest in the local schools.[48]*

In Shanghai, Eaton also supported a teachers college that trained educators to work in western China. Along with working with Shanghai Normal University to create a training program specifically for the region, Eaton also took groups of employees and people from the college there to build relationships and help improve the school districts.[49]

As Sandy Cutler explained, "[At Eaton], there has always been a tremendous focus on doing business right, and that strong culture and care for the individual employee has been one that fortunately has carried right through to today."

In 2011, for the fifth consecutive year, the Ethisphere Institute named Eaton one of the World's Most Ethical Companies, noting that "Eaton's promotion of a sound ethical environment shines within

Below: In 2006, Eaton opened a new plant in Jining City, China—the company's largest manufacturing facility in the entire Asia Pacific region (inset).

its industry and shows a clear understanding that operating under the highest standards for business behavior goes beyond goodwill and lip service and is intimately linked to performance and profitability."[50]

Eaton's presence in China has grown in leaps and bounds throughout the decade. In 2008, Eaton opened a new Asia Pacific headquarters in Shanghai.

### Leading by Sustainability

During a time of high fuel prices and tougher worldwide emissions regulations for trucks, Eaton consistently emphasized environmental sustainability in both its products and its operations. It set ambitious goals for reducing greenhouse gases in its plants and developed environmentally friendly components for customers in all of its markets, including truck and automotive, aerospace, electrical, and hydraulics.

In 2006, Eaton contracted with Rolls-Royce to supply components for its cleaner, quieter, environmentally friendly aircraft engine, and concur-

rently worked with vehicle suppliers on designing a diesel-electric hybrid power system for heavy-duty semi–tractors.[51]

"The world was becoming green in the sense that our customers were extremely sensitive to fuel consumption, to pollution," said Domenico Bertolino, retired vice president of Eaton's Valvetrain business. "So they were looking for better engines with better efficiency."

To stay ahead of the competition, Eaton's engine air management operations focused on quality and cutting-edge technology. Eaton strove to eliminate waste and developed smaller, more efficient engine components that drastically reduced emissions. "We thought our technology would be very helpful to the automotive companies, and it turned out that it was," said Larry Iwan, retired Eaton vice president of the Asia Pacific region.[52]

Eaton's sustainable vehicle projects included developing a diesel-electric powertrain for buses in China and the first hydraulic hybrid delivery truck, which was tested in the field in 2006 for United Parcel Service.[53]

Eaton's hybrid technology received international recognition in 2008, when it won a Blue Sky Award for Environmental Innovation and Technology from CALSTART, a transportation industry organization focusing on clean, energy-efficient technology. According to John Boesel, CALSTART president and CEO, the fact that Eaton was the only manufacturer producing both hybrid electric and hybrid hydraulic systems "was a driving force" in its selection. He explained, "Eaton truly deserves this credit for its pioneering clean transportation technology work and for the company's commitment to developing—and then taking to market—cutting-edge solutions for the transportation industry."[54]

Eaton had continued working on perfecting its hybrid technology for decades, even as the popular-

ity of hybrid technology waxed and waned throughout the industry over the years.[55] That dedication has paid dividends in the long run. Some of Eaton's hybrid powertrains can improve fuel economy by almost 50 percent. With the most successful trucking companies running up fuel tabs of $1 billion a year, hybrid engines can greatly affect a customer's bottom line.[56]

Like its vehicle components business, which had begun working on hybrid trucks for companies such as Coca-Cola and FedEx, Eaton's electrical business was also increasingly focused on sustainability. Eaton's electrical solutions were touted in the company's 2007 Annual Report as "contributing up to 40 percent of the total credit points that building owners need to achieve Leadership in Energy and Environmental Design (LEED) certification." A LEED-certified Electrical Group headquarters expansion in Pittsburgh opened in 2008.[57]

According to Thomas Gross, vice chairman and chief operating officer of the Electrical Group,

Hydraulic hybrid power systems are very efficient for vehicles that make frequent stops, such as this Eaton-designed hybrid United Parcel Service truck.

# HYBRID POWER SYSTEMS

IN 2000, EATON LAUNCHED ITS Hybrid Power Systems business unit. As a global leader in the electric, hydraulic, and vehicle components sectors, Eaton was primed to take advantage of its historical dedication to developing innovative fuel-saving technology. At the Detroit Auto Show in 2002, the company introduced Hydraulic Launch Assist, a breakthrough in fuel economy that facilitated the recovery of energy lost during vehicle braking. It would become part of Eaton's comprehensive hybrid powertrain development project.[1]

That year, FedEx and Environmental Defense announced that they had selected Eaton from more than 20 manufacturers to develop a new powertrain for an environmentally progressive commercial delivery vehicle. The vehicles were unveiled in 2003.[2] Soon after, Eaton received a $3.1 million contract from the U.S. Department of Energy to develop hybrid propulsion systems for trucks and other heavy-duty vehicles.[3]

The FedEx hybrid delivery trucks Eaton helped design began commercial operations in 2004 in Sacramento, California. Known as OptiFleet E7000s, the trucks produced 90 percent less particulate emissions than their conventional counterparts and 75 percent less smog-causing emissions. They also traveled 50 percent farther on a gallon of fuel, cutting total fuel costs by at least a third.[4]

The OptiFleet truck's powertrain combined an electric motor and a 4-cylinder diesel engine, which, thanks to the extra power the electric motor provided, was capable of operating more efficiently than a larger conventional 6-cylinder engine. The OptiFleet truck engine's state-of-the-art computer system automatically calculated the most efficient combination of electric and diesel power, taking into account current operating conditions and the

In 2004, FedEx became one of Eaton's biggest partners in hybrid-truck technology.

inefficient switching equipment and large transmission lines burn up energy before it reaches its destination. This can lead to anywhere between 25 percent to 40 percent loss of energy. As companies began to take notice, Eaton's expertise in energy efficiency has proven absolutely indispensible. The electrical industry's shift toward energy-efficient products happened practically overnight. "I've never before witnessed such a dramatic change," Gross said. "The orientation of our customers has gone through a revolution, and it's around sustainability."[58]

Eaton extended its sustainable philosophy to its own plants, as a member of the Business Roundtable's Climate RESOLVE initiative, Eaton pledged, using 2006 as the baseline, to reduce its greenhouse gas emissions by 18 percent by 2012. In Sumter, South Carolina, the company began designing a prototypical manufacturing site of the future that was greenhouse gas neutral. By 2007, demands of the driver. A particulate trap further cut down on emissions.

During the truck's regenerative braking phase, lithium ion batteries captured and stored the energy produced by slowing the vehicle—energy that was wasted in conventional braking systems. The stored energy could then provide electric power to the motor. Eaton's hybrid electric powertrain supplied all of the battery's electrical charging needs, avoiding the need for external plug-in stations.[5]

Eaton's hybrid power technology has proven an astounding success. Further testing showed that after a year or two on the road, the trucks continued to fulfill their environmental promise. In 2005, FedEx announced plans to add 75 more clean air trucks to its fleets in Texas and New York City.[6]

By January 2008, Eaton had added United Parcel Service, Coca-Cola, and PepsiCo to the growing customer list for its hybrid delivery trucks. Eaton's hybrid power systems were also utilized by a new fleet of 30 city buses in China, through a partnership with Beiqi Foton Motor Co. Ltd. and Guangzhou Yiqi Bus Co. Ltd. The buses were delivered during a ceremony that the U.S. Department of Commerce hosted as part of its Clean Energy Trade Mission to China and India.

The buses' remarkable fuel savings reached as high as 27 percent. They also reduced the amount of particulate and nitrogen oxide emissions in Guangzhou, a city of 12 million people.[7]

In 2009, newly inaugurated U.S. President Barack Obama previewed Eaton technology at the unveiling of a plug-in hybrid utility truck for Southern California Edison. The plug-in vehicle, which had a fuel economy that surpassed conventional trucks by up to 70 percent, was in its early test phase. Rechargeable via a power cord to a standard 120- or 240-volt electrical outlet, it was the first of five Eaton prototype trucks based on a Ford F-550 chassis.[8]

Eaton's plug-in hybrid technology proved popular right from the start. Later that year, Eaton announced that 378 more plug-in hybrids would be manufactured for more than 50 utility and municipal fleets in the United States. Each would have a range of at least 300 miles on a single charge.[9]

By the end of 2010, customers using Eaton hybrid power systems had collectively logged more than 100 million miles of service, reducing fuel consumption by 4 million gallons and harmful emissions by 40,000 metric tons. FedEx alone had reduced its fuel use by 200,000 gallons and carbon dioxide emissions by 2,000 metric tons—the equivalent of putting 300 fewer cars on the road each year. Across the globe, more than 2,400 Eaton hybrid systems were in use on delivery trucks, buses, refuse trucks, and delivery vehicles.[10]

Eaton also teamed up with Plug In Carolina to implement a new electric vehicle–charging network, with 80 Eaton charging stations expected to open throughout South Carolina by early 2011. The company launched a statewide tour on December 8, 2010, to celebrate the groundbreaking new charging network, one of the first statewide electric vehicle charging networks in the nation.[11]

the first year of reporting greenhouse gas reduction, Eaton made it halfway to its 2012 goal, cutting emissions by 9.2 percent.

In addition, Eaton has begun working with the U.S. Green Building Council to create guidelines for LEED-type certification for manufacturing sites as well as homes and buildings. Eaton has remained committed to not just minimizing its environmental impact, but actively improving the environment in the communities it serves.[59]

Eaton employees are proud of their company's dedication to sustaining the environment, and the company's ethical commitments help attract top talent across the industry. The company's environmental track record has resonated with many of the company's new recruits, especially Eaton's continued focus on developing sustainable products that can help customers drastically reduce their environmental impact. "It's about operating our factories in a sustainable manner, being mindful of our environ-

ment, maintaining clean water and clean air," said James McGill. "Our employees are actively engaged in a wide range of community support activities and Eaton has received recognition by many government organizations for our community support initiatives."

Above: California utility company PG&E partnered with Eaton in the development of a line of hybrid utility trucks.

Opposite: Emerging markets across the world have continued to provide Eaton with new opportunities to provide comprehensive solutions in the face of evolving infrastructure and rising energy costs. *(Photo ©iStockphoto.com/Robert Hunt.)*

### Ready for the Future

By 2007, for the first time, more than half of Eaton's revenues came from outside the United States. Eaton's strong focus on international growth would help the company through the difficult economic times to come.

The Electrical Group was Eaton's largest business, with eight new acquisitions between 2007 and 2008 with the largest of these acquisitions being the Moeller, Phoenixtec, and the MGE small systems business. Also during that period, Eaton acquired Cleveland-based Argo-Tech Corporation, a leader in high-performance aerospace engine fuel pumps and systems, airframe fuel pumps and systems, and ground fueling systems for both the commercial and military aerospace markets.[60]

Unfortunately, a deep recession hit the worldwide economy in the second half of 2008, and Eaton was forced to cut its workforce by more than 15 percent.[61] As part of the company's restructuring efforts during the recession, Eaton reorganized its global management structure, placing more emphasis on executive responsibility and accountability within its regional divisions, recognizing that a solid majority of the company's business now took place outside of U.S. borders. Eaton's international regions were empowered to make important decisions in a more timely manner, allowing the company to better compete on a global level. Also, to better capture internal operating and management synergies, in 2009, the company's internal operations were organized into two sectors: Electrical and Industrial.

Toward the end of the decade, Eaton would also acquire engineering services company EMC Engineers; CopperLogic Inc. an electromechanical systems manufacturer and representative of Moeller products in North America; and Wright Line Holding Inc. which specialized in IT data center thermal management.

According to Yannis P. Tsavalas, president of the Europe, Middle East, and Africa region, "We see the growth coming back, and we are ahead of our plans right now. For example, in Russia, we have created the Eaton Russia office for the business groups that are represented over there.

We're trying to leverage the Power of One Eaton and provide incremental resources from a corporate perspective to help achieve our growth objectives in Russia and help fulfill our growth potential over there. We're also expanding rapidly in the Middle East because that's another major growth area for us."

Thanks to Eaton's diversification efforts, its focus on its employees, and its investments in critical power management technologies, the company has fared better than many of its competitors and remains poised to take advantage of new global opportunities. In December 2010, Eaton stock

Left: Eaton, which has had a presence in Russia since the acquisition of Powerware in 2004, opened its corporate office in Moscow in October 2009.

Below: Employees and customers gather for the grand opening of Eaton's corporate office in Moscow.

broke all previous records, and analysts began predicting all-time record operating earnings per share by 2015. By 2015, Eaton also planned to obtain 60 percent of its revenues from outside the U.S., with 30 percent of all revenues coming from developing nations.

Eaton emerged a stronger company from the devastating global recession. Its performance in 2010 was even stronger than anticipated, confirming the prescience of Eaton's overall strategy as emerging economies led the global recovery.

"We outpaced the competitors during the market decline in both sales and operating profit, and on the way back up, we're doing the same," said William VanArsdale, president of Eaton's Hydraulics Group. "Everything considered, we did pretty well with what we were dealt."[62]

Rick Fearon, vice chairman and chief financial officer, added, "The growth that we're going to see out of this downturn will be a good mixture of organic and acquisition growth."[63]

As the world recovers from one of the worst recessions in a generation, Eaton has reaped the benefits of its long-term global strategy and the dedication of its loyal workforce. That has made a tremendous difference in terms of the company's enduring legacy. According to CEO Sandy Cutler:

*The recession of 2008 through 2009 was the worst recession that any of us have witnessed in our adult careers. In many respects, we were in a depression. There is nothing that parallels it, and even the emerging nations of the world were hit pretty hard. In that kind of terrible situation of no forward visibility, people really just were not sure what the future held. I think that Eaton employees around the world really rallied in a remarkable fashion. ... As a result, as the economy has started to come back, our markets were up about 11 percent in 2010, as part of the 20 percent we were down, we've recovered in 2010.*

*Over the last decade, we have worked hard to develop Eaton into a global power management enterprise and we have changed Eaton's mix of global businesses toward higher growth markets. Now approximately 75 percent of sales come from our Electrical, Hydraulics, and Aerospace businesses. We have also greatly expanded Eaton's international footprint with more than 55 percent of our sales outside the U.S. and more than 25 percent from emerging economies. This, along with our businesses having excellent balance across the economic cycle, firmly positions Eaton for continued profitable growth in the next decade and beyond.*

*As we set our sights on the future, we fully understand that power management will become more critical to our customers as the cost of extraction, processing, and distribution of energy will become more and more expensive and they will seek technologies to help them become more efficient. This need will fuel Eaton in the years ahead, and because of this we have set aggressive goals that reflect higher growth and performance for our company for the period of 2010 through 2015. They are:*

- *12 percent to 14 percent sales growth annually*
- *30 percent of sales from emerging markets*
- *20 percent earnings growth*
- *9 percent free cash flow as a percent of sales*
- *16 percent segment margins*
- *15 percent return on invested capital*

*It all adds up as Eaton enters its second century. The strategy is working, our momentum and the demand for our products are strong, and our global team of more than 70,000 is aligned, focused, and excited about our company's future.*[64]

# NOTES TO SOURCES

## Chapter One

1. "From Horseless Carriage to Palace Motor Car," *New York Times*, 12 January 1913.
2. *The History of Eaton Corporation 1911–1985* (Cleveland, Ohio: Eaton Corporation, 1985).
3. David D. Van Tassel and John J. Grabowski, editors, *The Encyclopedia of Cleveland History* (Bloomington and Indianapolis: Indiana University Press, 1987).
4. Beverly Rae Kimes, *Pioneers, Engineers, and Scoundrels: The Dawn of the Automobile in America* (Warrendale, Pennsylvania: SAE International, 2005).
5. *The Encyclopedia of Cleveland History.*
6. Viggo V. Torbensen, United States Patent: 1032517, 16 July 1921.
7. Viggo V. Torbensen, "The Torbensen Axle, Past and Present," *Torbensen Internal Opinion*, No. 1, 1918.
8. *The History of Eaton Corporation 1911–1985*, 1.
9. "The Torbensen Axle, Past and Present," 5.
10. *The History of Eaton Corporation 1911–1985*, 1.
11. E.L. Ludvigsen, *Eaton Yale & Towne: A Corporate Portrait* (New York: The Newcomen Society in North America, 1968).
12. "The Torbensen Axle, Past and Present," 6.
13. Mark S. Foster, *A Nation on Wheels: Automobile Culture in America Since 1945* (Belmont, California: Thomson Wadsworth, 2003), 349–350.
14. "The Torbensen Axle, Past and Present, 7.
15. *The History of Eaton Corporation 1911–1985*, 1.
16. Torbensen Axle 1917 Annual Report.
17. "The Torbensen Axle, Past and Present," 7.
18. *A Nation on Wheels*, 12.
19. *The History of Eaton Corporation 1911–1985*, 3.
20. "The Torbensen Axle, Past and Present," 7.
21. *The Encyclopedia of Cleveland History.*
22. "The Torbensen Axle, Past and Present," 7.
23. *The History of Eaton Corporation 1911–1985*, 4.
24. Howard Markt, "Systematizing Parts Manufacture," *Iron Trade Review*, 2 May 1918.
25. "Systematizing Parts Manufacture."
26. J.O. Eaton, "The Bigness of Little Things," *Torbensen Internal Opinion*, No. 1, 1918, 11.
27. "The Torbensen Axle: Past and Present," 7.
28. W. F. Rockwell, "To Our Employees," *Torbensen Internal Opinion*, No. 1, 1918, 3.
29. "Systematizing Parts Manufacture."
30. "Bloomerchinists," *Torbensen Internal Opinion*, No. 1, 1918, 10.
31. "Physical Care of Our Employees," *Torbensen Internal Opinion*, No. 1, 1918, 4.
32. "The Cafeteria," *Torbensen Internal Opinion*, No. 1, 1918, 22.
33. "Hurrah! Here They Are—The Champs," *Torbensen Internal Opinion*, No. 1, 1918, 12–13.
34. "Systematizing Parts Manufacture."
35. "The Bigness of Little Things," 11.
36. "A Nation on Wheels," 13.
37. Ibid., 12.
38. "War Motors Coming to Ports Overland," *New York Times*, 14 December 1917.
39. "News of Auto Trade Activities," *New York Times*, 3 March 1918.
40. Richard Wager, *Golden Wheels* (Cleveland, Ohio: John T. Zubal, Inc., 1986), 68–69.
41. *The History of Eaton Corporation 1911–1985*, 4.

42. Torbensen Axle 1917 Annual Report.
43. Ibid.
44. Republic Motor Truck Company 1917 Annual Report.
45. Ibid.
46. *The History of Eaton Corporation 1911–1985*, 5–6.
47. "Torbensen Axles Go to Japan," *Torbensen Internal Opinion*, No. 1, 1918, 18.

**Chapter One Sidebar:**
**J. O. Eaton**

1. *The History of Eaton Corporation 1911–1985* (Cleveland, Ohio: Eaton Corporation, 1985), 60.
2. Ibid.
3. Ibid., 61.
4. Ibid.
5. "Joseph O. Eaton, 75, Auto Industrialist, Dies," *Cleveland Plain Dealer*, 16 May 1949.
6. *The History of Eaton Corporation 1911–1985*, 61.
7. Ibid., 63.

**Chapter One Sidebar:**
**Viggo Torbensen**

1. "Memorial Record," pamphlet from Viggo Torbensen's funeral service, 1947.
2. "Memorial Record."
3. *The History of Eaton Corporation 1911–1985* (Cleveland, Ohio: Eaton Corporation, 1985), 64.
4. Ibid.
5. "V. V. Torbensen, Engineer, Is Dead," news clipping (publication unknown), January 1947.

**Chapter One Sidebar:**
**A Nation of Trucks**

1. *The History of Eaton Corporation 1911–1985* (Cleveland, Ohio: Eaton Corporation, 1985), 1.
2. Ibid.

3 "Transcontinental Delivery," Teamsters website, http://www.teamster.org/history/teamster-history/continental-delivery/.
4. Mark S. Foster, *A Nation on Wheels: Automobile Culture in America Since 1945* (Belmont, California: Thomson Wadsworth, 2003), 12.
5. Ibid.
6. "War Motors Coming to Ports Overland," *New York Times*, 14 December 1917.
7. "News of Auto Trade Activities," *New York Times*, 3 March 1918.
8. Richard Wager, *Golden Wheels*, (Cleveland: John T. Zubal, Inc., 1986), 68–69.
9. *The History of Eaton Corporation 1911–1985*, 4.

**Chapter Two**

1. Beverly Rae Kimes, *Pioneers, Engineers, and Scoundrels: The Dawn of the Automobile in America*, (Warrendale, Pennsylvania: SAE International, 2005), 421.
2. *Torbensen Internal Opinion*, No. 2, March 1919.
3. *Pioneers, Engineers, and Scoundrels*, 421.
4. *Torbensen Internal Opinion*, No. 2, March 1919.
5. Ibid.
6. "Torbensen Issue Attracts," *Cleveland Plain Dealer*, 5 April 1919.
7. A History of Eaton Corporation, 6.
8. Ibid.
9. *Pioneers, Engineers, and Scoundrels*, 429.
10. *The Eaton Story*, (Cleveland, Ohio: Eaton Manufacturing Company, 1957), 4.
11. Ibid., 9.
12. Ibid., 7.
13. "Plan Combine of Spring and Axle Concerns," *Cleveland Plain Dealer*, 11 February 1920.

14. *The History of Eaton Corporation 1911–1985* (Cleveland, Ohio: Eaton Corporation, 1985), 7.
15. "Eaton, Scott Named Parts Co. Receivers," *Cleveland Plain Dealer*, 1 September 1920.
16. Ibid.
17. *The History of Eaton Corporation 1911–1985*, 8.
18. "New Reorganization Plan," *New York Times*, 26 August 1922.
19. "Torbensen Plans Big Merger," *Cleveland Plain Dealer*, 11 April 1923.
20. "Eaton Again Heads Torbensen Axle," *Cleveland Plain Dealer*, 18 April 1922.
21. *The Eaton Story*.
22. John W. Hill, "Life Stories of Cleveland Firms: Eaton Manufacturing Company," *Clevelander*, October 1933, 12.
23. "Fisher Body, U.S. Steel, and Automotive Industry," The Encyclopedia of Cleveland History website, http://ech.cwru.edu/.
24. "Torbensen Plans Big Merger," *Cleveland Plain Dealer*, 11 April 1923.
25. *The History of Eaton Corporation 1911–1985*, 10.
26. "Life Stories of Cleveland Firms," 12.
27. *Eaton Plants and Products* (Cleveland, Ohio: Eaton Manufacturing Company, 1940).
28. *The History of Eaton Corporation 1911–1985*, 10.
29. Ibid.
30. Eaton Axle & Spring Company 1923 Annual Report.
31. *The History of Eaton Corporation 1911–1985*, 10.
32. *The History of Eaton Corporation 1911–1985*, 15.
33. "Wins Five-Year Axle Contract," *New York Times*, 2 September 1925.
34. *The History of Eaton Corporation 1911–1985*, 15.

35. Ibid.
36. Eaton Axle & Spring Company 1925 Annual Report.
37. "Life Stories of Cleveland Firms."
38. "Eaton Spring Company Gets Front Rank by New Purchase," *Cleveland Plain Dealer*, 18 June 1926.
39. Eaton Axle & Spring Company 1926 Annual Report, 3.
40. *The History of Eaton Corporation 1911–1985*, 65.
41. Eaton Axle & Spring Company 1927 Annual Report, 1.
42. "An Outline of Eaton's Growth," Company Timeline, 1948.
43. "Life Stories of Cleveland Firms," 12.
44. *The Eaton Story*, 16.
45. *The History of Eaton Corporation 1911–1985*, 12.
46. "Axle Company Buys Easy-On Cap Co.," *Cleveland News*, 6 July 1928.
47. *The History of Eaton Corporation 1911–1985*, 12.
48. *The Eaton Story*.
49. "Cleveland Makes the Parts," *Cleveland Press*, 9 January 1939.
50. Eaton Axle & Spring Company 1930 Annual Report, 2.

**Chapter Two Sidebar: Why Cleveland?**

1. *The History of Eaton Corporation 1911–1985* (Cleveland, Ohio: Eaton Corporation, 1985), 3.
2. "Automotive Industry," The Encyclopedia of Cleveland History website, http:// ech.cwru.edu/.
3. Ibid.

**Chapter Two Sidebar: Growth of an American Company**

1. Ludvigsen, E.L., *Eaton Yale & Towne: A Corporate Portrait* (New York: The Newcomen Society in North America, 1968), 12.

**Chapter Three**

1. Mark S. Foster, *A Nation on Wheels: The Automobile Culture in America Since 1945*, (Belmont, California: Thomson Wadsworth, 2003), 106–107.
2. Michael Smith, "UAW," Michigan History website, http://www.michiganhistory magazine.com/extra/2008/ septoct/uaw.html/.
3. Fred Kingsbury, "The News from Detroit," *New York Times*, 2 June 1929.
4. "Hoover Tells Auto Men Last Year's Sales Show No Cause for Pessimism," *New York Times*, 7 January 1931.
5. "Chrysler Salaries are Cut 10 Percent," *New York Times*, 4 July 1930.
6. "Auto Men Predict Prosperous Year," *New York Times*, 1 January 1930.
7. *The History of Eaton Corporation 1911–1985* (Cleveland, Ohio: Eaton Corporation, 1985), 13.
8. *The History of Eaton Corporation 1911–1985*, 13.
9. "Auto-Parts Makers on Way to Merger," *New York Times*, 21 February 1930.
10. Ibid.
11. *The History of Eaton Corporation 1911–1985*, 71.
12. "The Sodium-Cooled Valve," Wilcox-Rich Division of Eaton Manufacturing Co., archival document.
13. *The History of Eaton Corporation 1911–1985*, 71.
14. "Auto Parts Makers on Way to Merger."
15. *The History of Eaton Corporation 1911–1985*, 15.
16. "The Story of Eaton Manufacturing Company, Its Divisions and Subsidiaries," archival document, 30 November 1955.
17. "Eaton-Erb Foundry Buys Holley Assets," *Cleveland Plain Dealer*, 2 February 1932.
18. *The History of Eaton Corporation 1911–1985*, 13.
19. "Eaton Axle and Spring," *Chicago Journal of Commerce*, 11 May 1931.
20. "Eaton Axle to Add Unit," *New York Times*, 28 March 1931.
21. *The History of Eaton Corporation 1911–1985*, 14.
22. "Eaton Sees Many Mergers in Automobile Lines," *New York Times*, 26 March 1930.
23. "UAW."
24. T. H. Watkins, *The Great Depression: America in the 1930s* (Boston: Little, Brown & Company, 1993).
25. Eaton Manufacturing Company 1932 Annual Report.
26. Ibid.
27. Charles H. Larson, "Lack of Highway Facilities Real Problem for Dealers," *New York Times*, 5 January 1930.
28. John Lukacs, *A New Republic: A History of the United States in the Twentieth Century* (New Haven, Connecticut: Yale University Press, 2004), 106–107.
29. *The History of Eaton Corporation 1911–1985*.
30. "Motor Industry Code as Signed by Roosevelt," *New York Times*, 28 August 1933.
31. "Urges Abandoning New York Auto Show," *New York Times*, 31 December 1929.
32. "Car Buying Urged Now," *New York Times*, 10 November 1935.
33. "Early Auto Show to Steady Output," *New York Times*, 1 September 1935.
34. "Eaton Manufacturing Will Be Linked in Merger," archival news clipping, 29 September 1933.

35. "Quits Making Bumpers Here," *Cleveland Press*, 17 August 1934.
36. *The History of Eaton Corporation 1911–1985*, 16.
37. *The Great Depression*.
38. "UAW."
39. Ibid.
40. *The Great Depression*, 285.
41. "UAW."
42. Ibid.
43. *The Great Depression*.
44. Eaton Manufacturing Company 1934 Annual Report.
45. *The History of Eaton Corporation 1911–1985*, 15.
46. Eaton Manufacturing Company 1935 Annual Report, 3.
47. "Rain Fails to Check Auto Show Demand," *New York Times*, 8 November 1936.
48. "Motors Led the Way," *New York Times*, 8 December 1936.
49. "Auto Wages Total 800 Million a Year," *New York Times*, 14 February 1937.
50. Eaton Manufacturing Company 1936 Annual Report.
51. *The Great Depression*, 310.
52. Ibid., 311.
53. Eaton Manufacturing Company 1938 Annual Report.
54. *The History of Eaton Corporation 1911–1985*, 17.
55. "Engine Components History: 1938–1945," Eaton corporate archives.
56. *The History of Eaton Corporation 1911–1985*, 17.
57. Ibid.
58. Kenneth L. Austin, "Profits on Autos Rise 910 percent in Year," *New York Times*, 7 May 1939.
59. "Cleveland Makes the Parts," *Cleveland Press*, 9 January 1939.
60. David D. Van Tassel and John J. Grabowski, editors, *The Encyclopedia of Cleveland History* (Bloomington and Indianapolis: Indiana University Press, 1987).
61. "Cleveland Makes the Parts," Cleveland Press, 9 January 1929.
62. Eaton Manufacturing Company 1939 Annual Report.

**Chapter Three Sidebar: Helping Out Employees During Hard Times**

1. Logan Monroe interview, Eaton corporate archives.
2. Alexander M. Cutler, interview by Jeffrey L. Rodengen, digital recording, 31 July 2008, Write Stuff Enterprises, LLC.

**Chapter Four**

1. "Joseph O. Eaton, Auto Industrialist, Dies," *Cleveland Plain Dealer*, 16 May 1949.
2. Alan L. Gropman, *Mobilizing U.S. Industry in World War II* (Washington, D.C.: Institute for National Strategic Studies, 1996).
3. Eaton Manufacturing Company 1940 Annual Report.
4. "Engine Components History: 1938–1945," Eaton corporate archives, 1–2.
5. "234.5.2 Records of the Defense Plant Corporation," U.S. National Archives and Records Administration website, http://www.archives.gov/research/guide-fed-records/groups/234.html#234.5.2/.
6. *A Chronicle of the Automotive Industry in America, 1893 to 1949* (Detroit, Michigan: Automobile Manufacturers Association, 1949).
7. "24-Hour Limit Set on Defense Strike," *New York Times*, 15 January 1941.
8. "Engine Components History: 1938–1945," 2.
9. *The History of Eaton Corporation 1911–1985* (Cleveland, Ohio: Eaton Corporation, 1985), 19.
10. Ibid., 18.
11. *A Chronicle of the Automotive Industry in America, 1893 to 1949*.
12. *The History of Eaton Corporation 1911–1985*, 18.
13. Ibid., 19.
14. Ibid., 20–21.
15. "Engine Components History," 4.
16. Ibid., 8.
17. C. P. Trussell, "Autoists Warned No Tires Are Left, Own May Be Taken," *New York Times*, 6 March 1942.
18. Ibid.
19. Ibid.
20. Charles E. Egan, "Gasoline Rationing Ordered Widened to Entire Country," *New York Times*, 26 September 1942.
21. "Engine Components History," 22.
22. "Threefold Salvage Plan Carried on at Eaton," *Eaton News*, 3.
23. "War Plants Charge CMP Slows Output," *New York Times*, 18 March 1943.
24. *The History of Eaton Corporation 1911–1985*, 21.
25. "Engine Components History," 6.
26. "Buys U.S. War Plant," *New York Times*, 11 July 1945.
27. Eaton Manufacturing Company 1945 Annual Report.
28. Joseph Finkelstein, *The American Economy: From the Great Crash to the Third Industrial Revolution*, (Arlington Heights, Illinois: Harlan Davidson, Inc., 1992).
29. Eaton Manufacturing Company 1946 Annual Report.
30. Paul J. Melnick, "History of Dynamatic," Eaton corporate archives, 24 May 1974.

31. *The History of Eaton Corporation 1911–1985*, 21.
32. "History of Dynamatic."
33. "Eddy Current Harnessed by Winther Brothers at Dynamatic Plant," *Eaton News*, January 1947, 3–5.
34. "History of Dynamatic."
35. "Eddy Current Harnessed by Winther Brothers."
36. Charles Hickox interview, Eaton corporate archives.
37. Eaton Manufacturing Company 1947 Annual Report.
38. *The History of Eaton Corporation 1911–1985*, 21.
39. "Eaton's Biggest Campaign," *Tide*, 9 January 1948.
40. "New Use for an Old Principle," *BusinessWeek*, 28 February 1948.
41. Ibid.
42. Helene Lasch, "Advertising to Create Demand for Eaton Axles; Means More Jobs," *Eaton News*, September 1947, 15.
43. "Pump Division Expansion Program Continues," *Eaton News*, March 1948, 4.
44. *The Eaton Story*, (Cleveland, Ohio: Eaton Manufacturing Company, 1957).
45. *The History of Eaton Corporation 1911–1985*, 22.
46. "Eaton's Dynamatic Corporation Perfects Magnefluid Clutch," *Eaton News*, June 1948, 3.
47. "Saginaw Meets Customer Demand with New Foundry," *Eaton News*, May 1949, 5.
48. "24 Descendants Help J. O. Eaton Mark 75th Year," *Cleveland Plain Dealer*, 28 July 1948.
49. "Rites for Joseph O. Eaton, Industrialist, Set Tomorrow," *Cleveland News*, 16 May 1949.
50. "Joseph O. Eaton, Auto Industrialist, Dies," *Cleveland Plain Dealer*, 16 May 1949.

**Chapter Four Sidebar:
A Song Away from Home**

1. "Jim Writes Eaton War Song," *Eaton News*, July–August 1944, 16.

**Chapter Four Sidebar:
Remembering the Fallen**

1. Melissa Gerst, "From the Archives: Lt. Col. Marshall Fredericks, Sculptor and Military Man," MarshallFredericks.com website, http://www.marshallfredericks.com/?p=132/.
2. "Eaton Dedicates World War II Memorials at Seven Plants," *Eaton News*, September 1949, 8–9.
3. Jean Spenner, "Eaton Corp. War Monument to Head to Saginaw Valley State University," *Saginaw News*, 10 March 2008.

**Chapter Five**

1. "Eaton Manufacturing Company," *Ford Dealers News*, 1956.
2. Thomas F. Conroy, "Business Outlook Hinges on Smoothness in Shift to a Semi-War Economy," *New York Times*, 2 January 1951.
3. Eaton Manufacturing Company 1951 Annual Report.
4. Eaton Corporation 1950 Annual Report.
5. *Eaton News*, March 1951, 4.
6. "Eaton Parts in Jet Planes," *Eaton News*, November 1952, 8.
7. "Memo from Management," *Eaton News*, July 1951, 3.
8. "$1,000,000 Plant Expansion at Pump Division," *Eaton News*, July 1951.
9. "Eaton to Invest $8,000,000 in New Marion Plant and Equipment," *Eaton News*, June 1952.
10. Eaton Manufacturing Company 1952 Annual Report.
11. *This is Eaton*, promotional booklet, Eaton corporate archives, 1960.
12. Eaton Manufacturing Company 1953 Annual Report.
13. "Eaton's New Rear-Window Defroster," *Eaton News*, April 1952, 4.
14. "Eaton's New Ball Bearing Drive Screw in Production at Saginaw Division," *Eaton News*, January 1953.
15. Frank Rowsome Jr., "Magnetic Clutch Challenges," *Popular Science*, March 1954.
16. Ibid.
17. Eaton Manufacturing Company 1953 Annual Report.
18. "The Big Difference in Automotive Air Conditioning," *Eaton News*, September 1956, 6.
19. Eaton Manufacturing Company 1955 Annual Report.
20. "Increased Customer Demand Spells 'Expansion' for Heater Division," *Eaton News*, August 1956, 4.
21. "New Division Formed," *Eaton News*, January 1956, 6.
22. Ibid.
23. "A Step Ahead," *Eaton News*, September 1956, 4–5.
24. Ibid.
25. Eaton Manufacturing Company 1953 Annual Report.
26. "Fredric Flader Division," *Eaton News*, February 1957.
27. Ibid.
28. Ibid.
29. "A Step Ahead," 4–5.
30. Eaton Manufacturing Company 1957 Annual Report.
31. "Automotive Gear Works Inc.," June 1956, *Eaton News*, 4.
32. Ibid.

33. E. L. Ludvigsen, *Eaton Yale & Towne: A Corporate Portrait* (New York: The Newcomen Society in North America, 1968), 12.

34. "Automotive Gear Works Inc.," 4.

35. "From Managment's Point of View," *Eaton News*, July 1956, 4.

36. Eaton Manufacturing Company 1958 Annual Report, 3.

37. *Eaton Yale & Towne*, 13.

38. Damon Stetson, "Car Makers Face Vexing Problems; Map Major Steps," *New York Times*, 9 March 1958.

39. "Car Makers Take a Resigned View," *New York Times*, 13 June 1954.

40. "Labor: Fight for the Annual Wage," *Time*, 7 February 1955.

41. "Union Opens Chrysler Parleys, Expects to Win a Lay-Off Fund," *New York Times*, 28 June 1955.

42. Eaton Manufacturing Company 1955 Annual Report.

43. Eaton Manufacturing Company 1957 Annual Report; Eaton Manufacturing Company 1958 Annual Report.

44. Eaton Manufacturing Company 1957 Annual Report.

45. "3-Group Parley Saves Industry," *New York Times*, 7 August 1955.

46. Eaton Manufacturing Company 1957 Annual Report.

47. Eaton Manufacturing Company 1958 Annual Report.

**Chapter Five Sidebar: Fuller Manufacturing**

1. *The History of Eaton Corporation 1911–1985* (Cleveland, Ohio: Eaton Corporation, 1985), 72.

2. "Truck Components History," Eaton Corporation website, http://www.eaton.com/EatonCom/Markets/Truck/AboutTruck/History/index.htm/.

3. *The History of Eaton Corporation 1911–1985*, 72.

4. Thomas O'Boyle, interview by Jeffrey L. Rodengen, digital recording, 6 August 2008, Write Stuff Enterprises, LLC.

5. Ibid.

**Chapter Five Sidebar: E. Mandell de Windt**

1. *The History of Eaton Corporation 1911–1985* (Cleveland, Ohio: Eaton Corporation, 1985), 67–68.

2. Stephen Hardis, interview by Jeffrey L. Rodengen, digital recording, 31 July 2008, Write Stuff Enterprises, LLC.

3. E. Mandell de Windt, interview by Jeffrey L. Rodengen, digital recording, 22 July 2009, Write Stuff Enterprises, LLC.

4. *The History of Eaton Corporation 1911–1985*, 67–68.

5. Alexander M. Cutler interview by Jeffrey L. Rodengen, digital recording, 31 July 2008, Write Stuff Enterprises, LLC.

**Chapter Five Sidebar: International Growth**

1. Eaton Corporation 1957 Annual Report; Eaton Corporation 1958 Annual Report.

2. E. L. Ludvigsen, *Eaton Yale & Towne: A Corporate Portrait* (New York: The Newcomen Society in North America, 1968).

3. *The History of Eaton Corporation 1911–1985* (Cleveland, Ohio: Eaton Corporation, 1985), 31–32.

**Chapter Six**

1. Eaton Yale & Towne Inc. 1967 Annual Report.

2. *The History of Eaton Corporation 1911–1985* (Cleveland, Ohio: Eaton Corporation, 1985).

3. Ibid., 28.

4. Eaton Yale & Towne Inc. 1961 Annual Report.

5. "Why Does Eaton Go Abroad?" *Eaton News*, March 1962, 8–9.

6. Ibid.

7. Eaton Yale & Towne Inc. 1961 Annual Report.

8. *The History of Eaton Corporation 1911–1985*, 32.

9. "Eaton Acquires ENV Engineering of England," *Eaton News*, October 1962.

10. Eaton Yale & Towne Inc. 1962 Annual Report.

11. "Why Does Eaton Go Abroad?"

12. Ibid.

13. "Axle Scores Another Hit!" *Eaton News*, September 1961.

14. Eaton Yale & Towne Inc. 1961 Annual Report.

15. "The Big Challenge: Competition," *Eaton News*, April 1961.

16. "Eaton Acquires Cleveland Firm," *Eaton News*, July 1961, 4.

17. "Dill Manufacturing Company, *Eaton News*, August 1961, 8–10, 12.

18. Ibid.

19. "How to Handle a Parcel of Air," *Eaton News*, September 1961.

20. *The History of Eaton Corporation 1911–1985*, 28.

21. Eaton Yale & Towne Inc. 1963 Annual Report.

22. "Among the Newest Stars on the Eaton Map," *Eaton News*, January 1964, 10.

23. "New Research Center Dedicated to New Products, Ideas, and Processes," Eaton press release, 23 June 1961.

24. Eaton Yale & Towne Inc. 1963 Annual Report.

25. "Research," *Eaton News*, August 1961.

26. "$60 Million in Research Planned by Eaton Yale,"

*Cleveland Plain Dealer,*
24 February 1966.
27. Eaton Yale & Towne Inc.
1967 Annual Report.
28. "Air Bag Concept for Safety
Looks Good," *Steel,*
30 December 1968.
29. Bill Butler, interview by
Jeffrey L. Rodengen, digital
recording, 8 August 2008,
Write Stuff
Enterprises, LLC.
30. Vartanig G. Vartan,
"Happiness Could Be an Air
Bag," *New York Times,*
31 August 1969.
31. Bill Butler interview.
32. "The Revolution Continues,"
*Eaton News,*
February–March 1967.
33. "The Revolution Continues."
34. "*The History of Eaton
Corporation 1911–1985,*" 28.
35. Eaton Yale & Towne Inc.
1963 Annual Report.
36. "*The History of Eaton
Corporation 1911–1985,*" 28.
37. David D. Van Tassel
and John J. Grabowski,
editors, *The
Encyclopedia of Cleveland
History* (Bloomington
and Indianapolis:
Indiana University
Press, 1987), 378.
38. Eaton Yale & Towne Inc.
1964 Annual Report.
39. Eaton Yale & Towne Inc.
1965 Annual Report.
40. Eaton Yale & Towne Inc.
1967 Annual Report.
41. Eaton Yale & Towne Inc.
1964 Annual Report.
42. Eaton Yale & Towne Inc.
1964 Annual Report.
43. Eaton Yale & Towne Inc.
1965 Annual Report.
44. *The Role of the Multinational
Company in the World
Marketplace,* (Cleveland,
Ohio: Eaton Yale & Towne
Inc., 1969).
45. Eaton Yale & Towne Inc.
1967 Annual Report.

**Chapter Six Sidebar:
The Eaton Philosophy**

1. Steve Bartlett, "A History of the
Eaton Philosophy," internal
document, Eaton archives,
April 2010.
2. Joe Massey, interview by
Jeffrey L. Rodengen, digital
recording, 28 August 2009,
Write Stuff Enterprises, LLC.
3. "A History of the Eaton
Philosophy."
4. Donald N. Scobel, "Factory
Blues," *Harvard Business
Review,* November–December
1975, 132–142.
5. Ibid.
6. Joe Massey interview.

**Chapter Six Sidebar:
Global Business Units**

1. *The Role of the Multinational
Company in the World
Marketplace,* (Cleveland, Ohio:
Eaton Yale & Towne
Inc., 1969).
2. Eaton Yale & Towne Inc. 1968
Annual Report.
3. Eaton Yale & Towne Inc. 1968
Annual Report.

**Chapter Seven**

1. Eaton Corporation 1977
Annual Report.
2. *The Role of the Multinational
Company in the World
Marketplace,* (Cleveland, Ohio:
Eaton Yale & Towne Inc., 1969).
3. Eaton Yale & Towne Inc. 1968
Annual Report.
4. Ibid.
5. Ibid.
6. Ibid.
7. Eaton Yale & Towne Inc. 1969
Annual Report.
8. Eaton Yale & Towne Inc. 1970
Annual Report.
9. Eaton Yale & Towne Inc. 1969
Annual Report.
10. David D. Van Tassel and John
J. Grabowski, editors, *The

*Encyclopedia of Cleveland
History* (Bloomington and
Indianapolis: Indiana
University Press, 1987), 361.
11. Eaton Yale & Towne Inc. 1970
Annual Report.
12. *The History of Eaton
Corporation 1911–1985*
(Cleveland, Ohio: Eaton
Corporation, 1985), 37.
13. "Eaton Yale Planning to Buy
Char-Lynn Co. For 750,000 of
Common," *Wall Street Journal,*
December 24, 1970.
14. Bill Butler, interview by
Jeffrey L. Rodengen, digital
recording, 1 August 2008,
Write Stuff Enterprises, LLC.
15. Eaton Yale & Towne Inc. 1968
Annual Report.
16. Eaton Yale & Towne Inc. 1970
Annual Report.
17. *The History of Eaton
Corporation 1911–1985,* 37.
18. "Eaton Yale & Towne Expects
Sharp Fall in 2nd Quarter
Profit," *Wall Street Journal,*
30 June 1970.
19. Ibid.
20. *The History of Eaton
Corporation 1911–1985,*
37.
21. Eaton Yale & Towne Inc. 1970
Annual Report.
22. Ibid.
23. Eaton Corporation 1971
Annual Report.
24. "Eaton Expects Results in
1971 Will Fall Short of Earlier
Prediction, *Wall Street Journal,*
7 July 1971.
25. Michael C. Jensen, "Price
Rises Seen as Controls End,"
*New York Times,* 22 April
1974.
26. "1974 Review, 1975 Forecast,"
*Eaton Update for Managers,*
27 January 1975.
27. "Eaton Corp. To Post Sharp
Earnings Gains in Quarter
and Half," *Wall Street Journal,*
20 July 1972.
28. *The History of Eaton
Corporation 1911–1985,* 38.

29. Eaton Corporation 1973 Annual Report.
30. Ibid.
31. Ibid.
32. Ibid.
33. John Bendel, "Safety Brakes for Trucks—How Safe?" *New York Times*, 26 September 1975.
34. Eaton Corporation 1973 Annual Report.
35. Eaton Corporation 1974 Annual Report.
36. Eaton Corporation 1973 Annual Report.
37. Ibid.
38. *The History of Eaton Corporation 1911–1985*, 39.
39. Eaton Corporation 1974 Annual Report.
40. Eaton Corporation 1975 Annual Report.
41. Ibid.
42. Ibid.
43. Ibid.
44. *The History of Eaton Corporation 1911–1985*, 39.
45. Ibid., 41.
46. "Strategic Planning Lays Foundation for C-H Merger," *Eaton Update for Managers*, 27 June 1978.
47. Ibid.
48. Eaton Corporation 1977 Annual Report.
49. Eaton Corporation 1976 Annual Report.
50. Eaton Corporation 1977 Annual Report.
51. *The History of Eaton Corporation 1911–1985*, 42.
52. "Eaton Enters Engine Valve Business in Japan," *Eaton Update for Managers*, 10 July 1978.
53. *The History of Eaton Corporation 1911–1985*, 42.
54. "Eaton Advances 20 Places in the FORTUNE 500," *Eaton Update for Managers*, 27 September 1979.
55. Ronald Alsop, "Treading Warily," *Wall Street Journal*, 28 December 1979.

**Chapter Seven Sidebar:
Frank R. Bacon**

1. *Cutler-Hammer: 75-Year Perspective on the Future* (Milwaukee, Wisconsin: Cutler-Hammer, Inc., 1967), 17.
2. Ibid., 19.
3. Ibid., 21, 23.

**Chapter Seven Sidebar:
Cutler-Hammer**

1. *The History of Eaton Corporation 1911–1985* (Cleveland, Ohio: Eaton Corporation, 1985), 78–79.
2. Ibid.

**Chapter Eight**

1. Eaton Corporation 1981 Annual Report.
2. Ibid.
3. Ibid.
4. Eaton Corporation 1981 Annual Report.
5. "Eaton Poised for Profits from Its Shift to High Technology," *BusinessWeek*, 8 June 1981.
6. Eaton Corporation 1981 Annual Report.
7. "Eaton: Poised for Profits from Its Shift to High Technology."
8. Eaton Corporation 1981 Annual Report.
9. Eaton Corporation 1981 Annual Report.
10. Ibid.
11. Ibid.
12. Ibid.
13. Ibid.
14. Eaton Corporation 1982 Annual Report.
15. Ibid.
16. Stephen Hardis, interview by Jeffrey L. Rodengen, digital recording, 31 July 2008, Write Stuff Enterprises, LLC.
17. Eaton Corporation 1982 Annual Report.
18. Ibid.
19. Ibid.
20. Thomas O'Boyle, interview by Jeffrey L. Rodengen, digital recording, 6 August 2008, Write Stuff Enterprises, LLC.
21. Bob McCloskey, interview by Jeffrey L. Rodengen, digital recording, 1 August 2008, Write Stuff Enterprises, LLC.
22. Stephen Hardis interview.
23. Eaton Corporation 1982 Annual Report.
24. Eaton Corporation 1983 Annual Report.
25. Ibid.
26. Delinda Karle, "Prognosis Better for Smaller Eaton," *Automotive News*, 14 February 1983.
27. Ibid.
28. Eaton Corporation 1981 Annual Report.
29. Ibid.
30. Ibid.
31. Ibid.
32. "Eaton Poised for Profits from Its Shift to High Technology."
33. "Easier Driving's Goal of New Eaton Gearboxes," *Ward's Engine Update*, 1 August 1982.
34. Montieth M. Illingworth, "Road to Recovery," *Barron's*, 15 August, 1983.
35. Ibid.
36. Jeffrey J. Zygmont, "A Slimmer Eaton Poises for Future Growth," *Ward's Automotive Reports*, 3 October 1983.
37. Eaton Corporation 1985 Annual Report.
38. Eaton Corporation 1986 Annual Report.
39. "Eaton Increasing Role as 'Medium' Transmission Supplier," *Ward's Automotive Reports*, 1989.
40. Eaton Corporation 1988 Annual Report.
41. Ibid.
42. Eaton Corporation 1989 Annual Report.
43. Thomas O'Boyle interview, 6 August 2008.

44. Thomas O'Boyle, interview by Jeffrey L. Rodengen, digital recording, 6 August 2008, Write Stuff Enterprises, LLC.
45. Eaton Corporation 1980 Annual Report.
46. Ibid.
47. Eaton Corporation 1981 Annual Report.
48. Ibid.
49. Eaton Corporation 1985 Annual Report.
50. Eaton Corporation 1981 Annual Report.
51. Eaton Corporation 1982 Annual Report.
52. Eaton Corporation 1985 Annual Report.
53. Howard Gold, "Eaton Redux," *Forbes*, 3 June 1985.
54. Eaton Corporation 1986 Annual Report.
55. Eaton Corporation 1989 Annual Report.
56. "Eaton to Sell AIL, All Other Defense Electronics Units," *Aviation Week & Space Technology*, 2 November 1987.
57. "Rockwell Agrees to Buy Troubled Maker of B-1B Bomber's Electronic Jammers," *Wall Street Journal*, 8 December 1988.
58. "A Decade in Review," *Eaton Today*, February 1990.
59. John Miller, interview by Jeffrey L. Rodengen, digital recording, 1 August 2008, Write Stuff Enterprises, LLC.
60. Eaton Corporation 1984 Annual Report.
61. "A Decade in Review."
62. Eaton Corporation 1985 Annual Report.
63. Eaton Corporation 1986 Annual Report.
64. "1987 Archive Full List 1–100," FORTUNE® website, http://money.cnn.com/ magazines/fortune/ fortune500_archive/full/ 1987/.
65. "A Decade in Review."

66. Larry Oman, interview by Jeffrey L. Rodengen, digital recording, 8 July 2008, Write Stuff Enterprises, LLC.
67. Eaton Corporation 1987 Annual Report.
68. Eaton Corporation 1989 Annual Report.
69. "A Decade in Review."
70. "Motor of Future Is Goal at Lewis," *Cleveland Plain Dealer*, 13 April 1980.
71. Illmar Kains, "A New Page in EV History," *Automotive News*, 20 March 1989.
72. "Detroit Edison, Eaton Fuel EV Research," *Industry Week*, 1 June 1981.
73. Eaton Corporation 1982 Annual Report.
74. "A New Page in EV History."

**Chapter Eight Sidebar: Diversification**

1. John Miller, interview by Jeffrey L. Rodengen, digital recording, 1 August 2008, Write Stuff Enterprises, LLC.
2. Ted Wheeler, interview by Jeffrey L. Rodengen, digital recording, 14 July 2009, Write Stuff Enterprises, LLC.

**Chapter Eight Sidebar: Sandy Cutler**

1. Louis Uchitelle, "Ready for an Upturn. Not Ready to Spend," *New York Times*, 23 June 2002.
2. Ibid.
3. "Cutler to Become Chairman of Eaton Corporation," Eaton press release, 26 April 2000.
4. John Miller, interview by Jeffrey L. Rodengen, digital recording, 1 August 2008, Write Stuff Enterprises, LLC.
5. Victor A. Pelson, interview by Jeffrey L. Rodengen, digital recording, 16 July 2009, Write Stuff Enterprises, LLC.
6. John Miller interview.

**Chapter Nine**

1. Eaton Corporation 2000 Annual Report.
2. Eaton Corporation 1992 Annual Report.
3. Ibid.
4. Eaton Corporation 2000 Annual Report.
5. Annual Report 1994 Eaton Corporation.
6. Craig Arnold, interview by Jeffrey L. Rodengen, digital recording, 24 October 2008, Write Stuff Enterprises, LLC.
7. Eaton Corporation 1992 Annual Report.
8. Ibid.
9. Eaton Corporation 1993 Annual Report.
10. Ibid.
11. Ibid.
12. Eli Lustgarten, interview by Jeffrey L. Rodengen, digital recording, 4 May 2009, Write Stuff Enterprises, LLC.
13. Eaton Corporation 1993 Annual Report.
14. Stephen Hardis, interview by Jeffrey L. Rodengen, digital recording, 31 July 2008, Write Stuff Enterprises, LLC.
15. "Westinghouse History," Funding Universe website, http://www.fundinguniverse .com/company-histories/ Westinghouse-Electric- Corporation-Company- History.html/.
16. Stephen Hardis interview.
17. Eaton Corporation 1993 Annual Report.
18. John Holusha, "Company News; Westinghouse Sells a Unit to Eaton for $1.1 Billion," *New York Times*, 12 August 1993.
19. "Westinghouse History."
20. Ibid.
21. Stephen Hardis interview.
22. Eaton Corporation 1994 Annual Report.
23. Arnaldo Comisso, interview by Jeffrey L. Rodengen, digital

recording, 8 July 2008, Write Stuff Enterprises, LLC.

24. Jerry Whitaker, interview by Jeffrey L. Rodengen, digital recording, 25 July 2008, Write Stuff Enterprises, LLC.
25. Stephen Hardis interview.
26. Kristin Ohlson, "Into High Gear," *Inside Business*, September 1997.
27. Eaton Corporation 1996 Annual Report.
28. "Into High Gear."
29. Ibid.
30. Stephen Hardis interview.
31. Ibid.
32. "Eaton Forms Holding Company for China," Eaton press release, 20 November 1997.
33. "Eaton Corp. Joint Venture Agreement Signed," Eaton press release, 15 April 1996.
34. "Eaton in China," Eaton website, http://www .eaton.com/ecm/groups/ public/@pub/@eaton/ @corp/documents/ content/ct_234000.pdf
35. Ibid.
36. Eaton Corporation 1995 Annual Report.
37. C. B. Kim, interview by Jeffrey L. Rodengen, digital recording, 24 July 2008, Write Stuff Enterprises, LLC.
38. "Eaton Corporation to Open Automotive Assembly Plant in Korea," Eaton press release, 6 May 1997.
39. Eaton Corporation 1998 Annual Report.
40. Eaton Corporation 1994 Annual Report.
41. "Eaton, No. 2 in Hydraulics, to Buy Aeroquip-Vickers," *New York Times*, 2 February 1999.
42. "Eaton, No. 2 in Hydraulics, to Buy Aeroquip-Vickers."
43. "Aeroquip Corporation," Funding Universe website, http:// www.fundinguniverse.com/ company-histories/

Aeroquip-Corporation-Company-History.html/.
44. "Aeroquip Corporation."
45. *Our Industrial Heritage*, (Maumee, Ohio: Vickers, 1988).
46. Thomas W. Gerdel, "Transformation at Eaton," *Cleveland Plain Dealer*, 23 June 2000.
47. Jeff Finch, interview by Jeffrey L. Rodengen, digital recording, 10 July 2008, Write Stuff Enterprises, LLC.
48. "Transformation at Eaton."
49. Ibid.
50. Craig Arnold Interview.
51. "Transformation at Eaton."
52. Craig Arnold interview.
53. Ibid.
54. Bill Blausey, interview by Jeffrey L. Rodengen, digital recording, 31 July 2008, Write Stuff Enterprises, LLC.
55. Ibid.
56. Eaton Corporation 1999 Annual Report.
57. Eaton Corporation 2000 Annual Report.
58. Ibid.
59. Ibid.

**Chapter Nine Sidebar: Eaton Business System**

1. "Eaton Business System," Eaton website, http://www.eaton.com/ EatonCom/OurCompany/ About Us/ CorporateInformation/ EatonBusinessSystem/ index.htm/.
2. Susan J. Cook, interview by Jeffrey L. Rodengen, digital recording, 6 July 2009, Write Stuff Enterprises, LLC.
3. "Same Goal, New Enabling Tool: EBS," *Eaton Today*, January 1999.
4. Ibid.
5. Ibid.
6. Ibid.

7. Eli Lustgarten, interview by Jeffrey L. Rodengen, digital recording, 4 May 2009, Write Stuff Enterprises, LLC.
8. Susan J. Cook interview.
9. Yannis Tsavalas, interview by Jeffrey L. Rodengen, digital recording, 4 September 2008, Write Stuff Enterprises, LLC.
10. Gary L. Tooker, interview by Jeffrey L. Rodengen, digital recording, 14 July 2009, Write Stuff Enterprises, LLC.
11. Susan J. Cook interview.

**Chapter Nine Sidebar: Accelerated Growth**

1. Alexander M. Cutler, interview by Jeffrey L. Rodengen, digital recording, 31 July 2008, Write Stuff Enterprises, LLC.
2. Ibid.
3. Ibid.

**Chapter Ten**

1. Eaton Corporation 2001 Annual Report.
2. Eaton Corporation 2000 Annual Report.
3. "Eaton Corporation—CHMN & CEO—Interview," CNBC/Dow Jones Business Video, 17 July 2001.
4. "Eaton Corporation to Take Its Semiconductor Business Public," Eaton press release, 26 April 2000.
5. Stephen Buente, interview by Jeffrey L. Rodengen, digital recording, 19 August 2008, Write Stuff Enterprises, LLC.
6. Ibid.
7. Ibid.
8. Randy Carson, interview by Jeffrey L. Rodengen, digital recording, 20 August 2008, Write Stuff Enterprises, LLC.
9. "Eaton to Acquire Boston Weatherhead Business from Dana," Eaton press release, 1 October 2002.
10. Ibid.

11. "Eaton Announces Actions to Integrate Boston Weatherhead Business," Eaton press release 14 January 2003.
12. Eaton Corporation 2003 Annual Report; "Eaton Reports Fourth Quarter Net Income Of $1.71 Per Share, Up 8 percent," Eaton press release, 22 January 2008.
13. Eaton Corporation 2003 Annual Report.
14. Eaton Corporation 2004 Annual Report.
15. Susan J. Cook, interview by Jeffrey L. Rodengen, digital recording, 13 January 2011, Write Stuff Enterprises, LLC.
16. Ibid.
17. Eaton Corporation 2001 Annual Report.
18. "Eaton Reaches Agreement to Purchase Aerospace Fluid and Air Division of Cobham plc," Business Wire, 13 September 2005.
19. "Eaton to Purchase Aerospace Division of PerkinElmer Inc.," Eaton press release, 12 October 2005.
20. Brad Morton, interview by Jeffrey L. Rodengen, digital recording, 25 July 2008, Write Stuff Enterprises, LLC.
21. Ibid.
22. "Cessna Selects Eaton As the Complete Fuel Supplier on the New Citation Columbus Business Jet," Eaton press release, 11 July 2008.
23. "Eaton to Acquire Electrical Division of Delta plc," Eaton press release, 9 December 2002.
24. Ibid.
25. Frank Campbell, interview by Jeffrey L. Rodengen, digital recording, 21 January 2011, Write Stuff Enterprises, LLC.
26. "Eaton Completes Purchase of the Moeller Group,"Eaton press release, 4 April 2008.
27. "Company History," Moeller Group website, http://

www.moeller.net/ en/company/profile/ history/index.jsp/.
28. Frank Campbell interview.
29. Thomas Gross, interview by Jeffrey L. Rodengen, digital recording, 1 July 2009, Write Stuff Enterprises, LLC.
30. Jeff Krakowiak, interview by Jeffrey L. Rodengen, digital recording, 4 August 2009, Write Stuff Enterprises, LLC.
31. Billie K. Rawot, interview by Jeffrey L. Rodengen, digital recording, 11 August 2008, Write Stuff Enterprises, LLC.
32. "A Bargain on 18 Wheels," Barron's, 4 June 2008.
33. Randy Carson interview.
34. Bill Hartman, interview by Jeffrey L. Rodengen, digital recording, 1 August 2008, Write Stuff Enterprises, LLC.
35. James McGill, interview by Jeffrey L. Rodengen, digital recording, 17 August 2010, Write Stuff Enterprises, LLC.
36. Mark M. McGuire, interview by Jeffrey L. Rodengen, digital recording, 14 August 2010, Write Stuff Enterprises, LLC.
37. Ibid.
38. Eaton Corporation 2004 Annual Report; Eaton Corporation 2008 Annual Report.
39. Ibid.
40. Dan Shingler, "Eaton's China Presence Burgeoning," Crain's Cleveland Business, 1 December 2008.
41. Ibid.
42. Ibid.
43. James McGill interview.
44. Eaton Corporation 2006 Annual Report.
45. "Eaton Mobilizes Dedicated Customer Support in Wake of Hurricane Katrina," NEMA press release, 16 September 2005.
46. Eaton Corporation 2006 Annual Report.

47. Barry Doggett interview, interview by Jeffrey L. Rodengen, digital recording, 31 July 2008, Write Stuff Enterprises, LLC.
48. Ibid.
49. Ibid.
50. "Eaton Named One of the World's Most Ethical Companies in 2010," Eaton press release, 2 April 2010.
51. Eaton Corporation 2006 Annual Report.
52. Larry Iwan, interview by Jeffrey L. Rodengen, digital recording, 11 August 2008, Write Stuff Enterprises, LLC.
53. Eaton Corporation 2006 Annual Report.
54. "Eaton Wins CALSTART 2008 Blue Sky™ Award for Environmental Innovation and Technology," Eaton press release, 24 June 2008.
55. James Sweetnam, interview by Jeffrey L. Rodengen, digital recording, 11 August 2008, Write Stuff Enterprises, LLC.
56. Ibid.
57. Eaton Corporation 2007 Annual Report.
58. Thomas Gross interview.
59. Joe Wolfsberger, interview by Jeffrey L. Rodengen, digital recording, 1 August 2008, Write Stuff Enterprises, LLC.
60. Eaton Corporation 2007 Annual Report.
61. Eaton Corporation 2008 Annual Report.
62. William R. VanArsdale, interview by Jeffrey L. Rodengen, digital recording, 19 August 2010, Write Stuff Enterprises, LLC.
63. Rick Fearon, interview by Jeffrey L. Rodengen, digital recording, 27 August 2010, Write Stuff Enterprises, LLC.
64. Alexander M. Cutler, interview by Jeffrey L. Rodengen, digital recording, 6 August 2010, Write Stuff Enterprises, LLC.

**Chapter Ten Sidebar:
Regionalization**

1. Jeffrey M. Krakowiak, interview by Jeffrey L. Rodengen, digital recording, 4 August 2009, Write Stuff Enterprises, LLC.
2. Alexander M. Cutler, interview by Jeffrey L. Rodengen, digital recording, 6 August 2010, Write Stuff Enterprises, LLC.

**Chapter Ten Sidebar:
Hybrid Power Systems**

1. "Eaton Corporation Unveils Breakthrough Fuel Saving Technology at 2002 North American International Auto Show," Eaton press release, 7 January 2002.
2. "FedEx Express Introduces Hybrid Electric Truck," AScribe Newswire, 20 May 2003.
3. "U.S. Department of Energy Awards Contract to Eaton for Truck Hybrid System Development," Business Wire, 20 June 2003.
4. "New FedEx Hybrid Electric Trucks to Begin Service," Business Wire, 30 March 2004.
5. Ibid.
6. "FedEx Announces Plans to Add Up to 75 'Clean Air' Hybrid Trucks to Fleet," Business Wire, 22 April 2005.
7. "Eaton Corporation Introduces Its First Commercially Available Hybrid Power System in China with Beiqi Foton Bus Company and Guangzhou Yiqi Bus," Business Wire, 14 January 2008.
8. "President Obama Previews First Plug-In Hybrid Electric Utility Truck System Developed by Eaton and EPRI for Southern California Edison," Eaton press release, 19 Mary 2009.
9. "Eaton Corp. To be Part of Nation's Largest Deployment of Commercial Hybrid Vehicles," *Crain's Cleveland Business*, 12 August 2009.
10. "Eaton Hybrid Systems Achieve 30 Million Miles of Service Worldwide," Eaton press release, 3 March 2010.
11. "Plug In Carolina and Eaton Join for Tour to Kick Off Electric Vehicle Charging Network in South Carolina,"TradingMarkets.com website, http://www.tradingmarkets.com/news/stock-alert/etn_plug-in-carolina-and-eaton-join-for-tour-to-kick-off-electric-vehicle-charging-network-in-south-caro-1362981.html/.

# INDEX

*Page numbers in italics indicate photographs.*